"Sun Wu's Art of War" and the Art of Business Management

by
Li Shijun, Yang Xianju
and *Qin Jiarui*

Translated from Chinese by *Mou Xudian*

Hai Feng Publishing Co.

The translation is contributed by
the China Southwest Book Corporation,
Chongqing, Sichuan

© **Hai Feng Publishing Co.**
ISBN 962-238-173-1

Published by
Hai Feng Publishing Co.
Rm. 1502 Wing On House,
71 Des Voeux Rd., C.
Hong Kong.

Printed by
Friendly Printing Co., Ltd.
Flat B1, 3/F Luen Ming Hing Ind. Bldg.,
36 Muk Cheong St., Tokwawan,
Kowloon, Hong Kong.

First Edition January 1990
Second Edition September 1994

HF-147-P

Published & Printed in Hong Kong

Dedicated to
Pioneer-entrepreneurs – enthusiasts
for applying Sun Wu's Art of War
to business management

Contents

Introduction

Authors of this book are attempting to introduce some of the scientific ideas and methods expounded in the Chinese classic "Sun Wu's Art of War" (or "Sun Zi's Art of War", "Master Sun's Art of War") into modern business management, in order to blaze a new path in improving China's business management and administration and working out a Chinese-style system of scientific business management.

One may ask: could such a proposition—to apply "Sun Wu's Art of War" (hereafter referred to as "Sun Zi", formerly transliterated as "Sun Tzu") to business management, which means to link an ancient classical treatise on war up with modern business management and, what is more, with the supposed founding of a Chinese-style system of scientific business management—be in conformity with the basic tenets of Marxism-Mao Zedong-Thought? Wouldn't there be a most improbable tie-up of two completely irrelevant things? We would like to set forth our views in this connection for all who concern themselves with this problem to consider.

I

Fundamentally, the guiding principle for founding a scientific system of business management with Chinese characteristics is Marxism-Mao Zedong-Thought. This, however, by no means exclude the possibility of applying the scientific ideas contained in "Sun Zi" to business management. In his speech at the meeting in commemoration of the centennial of Karl Marx's death, Hu Yaobang, General Secretary of the Chinese Communist Party, put it well: "The wrong tendency of isolating Marxism from the cultural fruits of mankind and setting them against each other should certainly be opposed." Since Marxism-Mao Zedong-Thought is the crystallization of the cultural and scientific riches of humanity and the ideological weapon for perceiving and transforming the world, and "Sun Zi" has been a brilliant gem in the treasurehouse of China's ancient culture to be worked to serve the development of China's new national culture, wouldn't it very well accord with the basic demands of Marxism-Mao Zedong-Thought to explore "Sun Zi"'s rich legacy under the guidelines of Marxism-Mao Zedong-Thought to help improve our business management and promote China's modernization drive?

In our view, "Chinese characteristics" is what we should stress in developing a Chinese-style system of scientific business management. We should, under the guidance of Marxism-Mao Zedong-Thought, absorb things scientific from abroad while, what is more essential, keeping in view China's realities. Only in this way can a Chinese system of scientific business management take root in the fertile soil of China, a country with a long history of brilliant civilization, a priceless cultural legacy and a treasurehouse of experience gained in the decades-long revolution and construction since the founding of the People's Republic of China in 1949. Therefore, we appreciate the role of the study of business management in the light of the scientific ideas of "Sun Zi" in developing a scientific system of business management with Chinese characteristics.

II

"Sun Wu's Art of War", also referred to as "Sun Zi" (formerly transliterated as "Sun Tzu"), or "Sun Zi's Art of War", or "Sun Zi of Wu's Art of War", was written in the fifth century B.C. when the historical period known as "Spring and Autumn" (770-476 B.C.) was coming to an end. It is China's and also the world's most ancient work on the theory of war.

The author of this classic of military science was Sun Wu Zi, or Master Sun Wu.

A native of the state of Qi, Sun Wu lived in the late years of the "Spring and Autumn" period. As it was in the state of Wu that he displayed the brilliance of his military talents and performed his military feats, he was also called Sun Zi (or Master Sun) of Wu. The exact dates of his birth and death still remained to be verified; we only know that he was, roughly speaking, a contemporary of Kong Zi (Confucius). In 512 B.C. he exiled himself from the state of Qi to the state of Wu and was recommended by Wu Zixu, a high-ranking official of the state of Wu, to Helu, King of the state of Wu. He compelled the admiration of the King by his astonishingly superior arguments, his views radiant with genius and the magnificant 13-chapter "Art of War" which he had brought with him, and was appointed by the King to a very important post. Together with Wu Zixu, Sun Wu now assisted the King in running the state and training the army, thus contributing to the rise of the state of Wu. As is recorded in ancient annals, Sun Wu made outstanding military exploits in his 30-year military career from 512 B.C. when he was called in by the King of Wu to 482 B.C. when he succeeded in getting the state of Wu to the position of a hegemony in place of the state of Jin. A great military theorist and strategist, Sun Wu made great achievements in the theory and practice of war. He has been revered in Japan as a "war sage", the way Confucius has been worshipped there as a "learning sage".

The monumental work that is "Sun Zi" (formerly transliterated as "Sun Tzu") is a summary of the basic concepts and principles of army management and the experience of warfare which were the assets of the slaveholder class and the emerging landlord class of the late years of the "Spring and Autumn" period and the years before them. The work puts emphasis on the great importance of honest and enlightened government, careful investigation and study and the analysis of the conditions of the foe, and gives prominence to the commander's capability of reacting to the circumstances in war, or, in other words, winning victory by utilizing the conditions of the foe. The book also elaborates on the role of and the requirements for a commander. "Sun Zi" exerted immense influence on the development of the military ideas of ancient China and occupies an important place in the world's war history, being reputed as "the originator of Oriental military science", "the Number One military work of ancient world,"and "the Holy Code of military science." Thirteen chapters of "Sun Zi" have been handed down to us, namely: "Reckoning," "Waging War," "The Strategy of Attack," "Position," "Momentum," "The Void and the Solid," "Contention for Advantages," "Endless Tactical Adaptations," "Marches," "Terrain," "The Nine Varieties of Battle-ground," "Attack by Fire" and "Espionage."

As a historic work on military science, "Sun Zi" presents an all-embracing, well-knit and profound system of military thinking in a masterpiece revealing the law of war. Moreover, there are quite a few praiseworthy political viewpoints in "Sun Zi." The naive materialist and dialectical concepts the book presents occupy an important position in the history of Chinese philosophy, and the literary worth of "Sun Zi" with its brilliant exposition, compact structure, sonorous and forceful language and colourful style of writing has been highly valued. The 13-chapter treatise of merely around 8,000 characters gives such learned debates in battle of wits and such meticulours descriptions of the valiant hand-to-hand fights that from the reading of its first paragraphs one feels as if witnessing how a monarch and his officials were plotting in the palace and hearing how a battle was raging on with shouts and clanks—a superb presentation of life itself!

III

How could one possibly apply the concepts of "Sun Zi", an ancient treatise on warfare to the study of the problems of business management today? Might there be any links between the two?

To give an answer to these questions, let us discuss first what management is. Management as such may fall into two categories: management of production in its general sense and management of business. Studied in the general sense of the word, management, a term with a broad connotation, involves all joint efforts of men. By management are meant the activities intended for fulfilling a task which none of the people joining each other in their common effort can accomplish on his own. So management is needed for an effective division of labour and cooperation and an effective use of resources including manpower, materials, finance, technology, information and time. In a sense, management is a kind of resources, too, and one serving as a medium for all other resources by the reason that, like other kinds of resources such as time, it would be meaningless without men's activities, and when we say that management serves as a medium for all other resources, we mean that without management, resources in human activities would fail to play their roles and there would be no effective integration of different kinds of resources. Regarding management, Karl Marx made his penetrating statement: "All combined labour on a large scale requires, more or less, a directing authority, in order to secure the harmonious working of the individual activities, and to perform the general functions that have their origin in the action of the combined organism,... (K. Marx, "Capital", Eng. ed. Moscow, 1959, Vol 1, p. 106) Management required by the process of joint labour is of universal significance.

Management is a kind of practice. It is as old as the conscious activities of mankind and human civilization. In the millennia of their activities people have been accumulating and summarizing their ideas and methods of planning, organization, control, direction, coordination and policy-making in the field of politics, warfare, economy, culture, religion, etc. In a word, they have been improving their management. Examples: Without an outstanding talent of men for management, i.e., for planning, organization, etc., without their rich experience in management, the gigantic engineering feat of building the Great Wall undertaken by Chin Shi Huang (or First Emperor of Chin who reigned 246-210 B.C.) would not have been successful. And the unification of measurement system and the standardization of the written language, enforced by Chin Shi Huang, was none other than a kind of standardization of management. Also, the Dujiang Dam irrigation system built under Li Bin and his son in the Warring States period (476-221 B.C.) embodied to some extent the naive ideas of systems analysis. So it can be seen that knowledge of management has been gained and crystalized in the process of people's joint activities.

Management is as much an art as a science. It is a science in the sense that management always entails a scientific approach to planning a move as accurately as possible by precise measurement, in accordance with the laws of Nature and economic activities. It is an art, because the resources available, the conditions and various factors related to "oneself" and "one's adversaries" which are linked to management are always changing, and an effective management is always a random one, one that varies with the circumstances.

Business management has a dual nature, being the unity of management of production and management of relations of production. Good business management involves both scientific organization of production and proper management in the field of the relations of production and the superstructure of the society. This is also true of employing troops in war. In order to win a battle, one has to know both oneself and the enemy and act in keeping with the circumstances, "sitting within a command tent and devising strategies that will assure victory a thousand li away", and at the same time realize a good management of the troops themselves and handle properly the relations inside the troops and those of the troops with other people by "civil virtues" and "martial authority" in a just cause one is dedicated to with a full understanding of the "Right Way".

Not until just around a hundred years ago did people begin to study and promote management as a science systematically. It has gradually taken shape along with the birth and development of capitalism. The disintegration of the handicraft production, the emergence of large-scale production by machinery and the formation of the factory system caused the decline of individual, simple labour and brought forth large-scale cooperation as the main form of labour. As command, coordination and organization are indispensable for a large-scale production, knowledge of management accumulated in the millennia of civilization and found scattered in the realms of economic, technological, military and other sciences began to be applied in that production, evolving an independent science of management. As coordinated labour is developed to the fullest in the large-scale production of the enterprises, the need for proper management is more urgent, and ideas of management assert themselves more clearly and the managerial behaviour manifests itself more systematically than anywhere else, it is only natural that the science of management is known first of all as the science of business management.

The science of business management presents itself as a conglomeration of knowledge from all related subjects including military science. So it follows that the basic ideas of business management, once refined and distilled, can be of universal significance for all other scientific activities. It is generally accepted that the science of business management came into being at the turn of the century. Various approaches have been evolved ever since—F. Taylor's scientific management and organization theory; the managerial process approach which takes management as a process; the operational approach which considers operation as the key to management; the decision theory approach which takes management as decision-making; the empirical approach which holds that management is where the experience of all activities go; the mathematical approach which advocates management by means of mathematical theorems and methods; the social systems approach which apply sociological theses to the study of business management; the behaviourist approach which takes a psychological and sociological view toward the study of business management, and the list could go on and on. What is noteworthy is that as early as nearly 2,000 years ago our forebears already know classification of management to which testifies the "Journal of Literature" of "Han Shu" ("History of the Western Han Dynasty" (206 B.C.-A.D., 24)) which divided the pre-Han military works into four categories; strategist, operational, Yin-Yang-oriented,* and crafts related. The first two categories represented a likeness of the views of the school of management as decision-making and those of the school of managerial process respectively.

From the above-mentioned we can see that management as such has spanned thousands of years and embraced all walks of life without exception. Business management can draw upon the ancient cultural heritage including ideas of military science, and in our times military science in turn can absorb ideas of business management. Here we have a blood relationship between the two.

Nowadays it can easily be seen that business management has

---

*In ancient Chinese philosophy, Yin and Yang represented two opposing elements of nature, the former femine and negative, the latter masculine and positive.—*Trans.*

in fact adopted in profusion the managerial ideas, organizational methods and art of leadership from the field of military affairs. For example, the idea "to dispatch an army for a just cause" and emphasis on the device of strategies and the study of tactics find their expression in business management. Quite a few terms now in usage in business management have been taken from military terminology: "headquarters" of the enterprise standing for its leading body; "command system in production" standing for production management organization; "strategic decision", "quotations strategy" and many others. Discussing problems concerning business management, Karl Marx borrowed on many occasions military concepts of management to make his point. Touching on the necessity of management in business, he wrote, "An industrial army of workmen, under the command of a capitalist, requires, like a real army, officers (managers), and sergeants (foremen, overlookers),..." (K. Marx, 'Capital", Eng. ed., Moscow, 1959, Vol. 1, p. 332) And the pyramidic structure of management and the installation of sections and offices performing advisory functions in matters of management are things imitated from the field of military affairs.

What is typical of the interaction between military science and management is the fact that operational research find its wide application in business management and the management of some major scientific research projects and major engineering projects. For instance, the application of operational research to the solution of problems of systems engineering and network planning technology and the successful application of the scientific knowledge of systems engineering and operational research to the U.S. "Manhattan Project" developing the atomic bomb in the 1940s and the Apollo Missions landing man on the moon in the 1960s.

So far we have discussed the relationship between the art of war and management in the general sense of the latter. Now let us deal with the problem from the standpoint of business management.

What distinguishes business management from management in general is that the former extends management from the production process to the realm of commodity circulation, turns its attention from sales based on production to production based on sales prospects, shifts its stress from current management onto management of the future, and aims at enhancing economic results rather than merely fulfiling production tasks. In handling business management, a manager has to attach more importance to market, competition, and efficacy that in handling production management, which means that decision-making and scheming for promoting sales are to stand out as salient points in business. As the military treatise "Sun Zi" emphasizes strategy-devising and scheming for counteraction, business management can very well benefit from "Sun Zi"'s concepts and basic tenets, and they have much in common in these questions.

Although wars have never stopped in the world after World War II, the main battles being fought in these days are economic rather than military ones. In the capitalist world, "market is battlefield" and "competition is war". Competition between various enterprises, being an undeclared economic "war", is just as much a life-and-death struggle as a war between armies is. This special war represents a very complicated struggle for market and for customers. Before World War II, with supplies being not so plentiful and competitors being not so numerous, the consumers bought what the enterprises turned out and the entrepreneurs kept their control over the market, mainly by increasing output. Things, however, have changed since the 1950s when the rapid advance of science and technology had caused enormous expansion of production, commodity supply had greatly outstripped the demand of the consumers, the contradiction between production and consumption had sharpened, competitions for market had become increasingly fierce, and the days had gone forever when a few enterprises held sway over the market. In our days, the contradiction between production and consumption finds its expression not so much in the quantity of the products as in their quality and variety. And the competition between the entrepreneurs involves not only the quantities of the commodities but also tactics of promoting sales. In order to live up to the demands of such a "war", the capitalist nations and the capitalists are vigorously seeking ways to victory. The penetrating views contained in "Sun Zi", a military treatise of ancient China, therefore, call the attention of some capitalists who want to get from it some tips for survival in a fierce competition.

As for China, while implementing a policy of opening to the outside world, trading with foreign capitalists and utilizing the foreign funds and advanced technology for her own interests, which is a necessity, she has to prevent herself from being cheated in the business intercourses with the capitalist countries and at the same time win the competition with businessmen abroad by getting her commodities into the world market. Therefore, it is imperative for us Chinese to study "Sun Zi" and make this "heirloom" of ours serve our cause.

So far as domestic situation is concerned, China's modernization program requires that we do a good job of the management of our enterprises, promote production and sales, enhance the quality of the enterprises and their economic results, and carry on socialist competition. Our enterprises now face a serious challenge. Socialist competition, differ from the competition between capitalist enterprises in nature as it may, is also characterized by antagonism inherent in competition in general. Thus, it is competition that forces the enterprises to turn out a maximum of the products to meet the needs of the market, increase varieties of the products, raise their quality and lower their costs and improve sales service. And it is again competition that forces leaders of an enterprise to define clearly the rights and responsibilities of each of them and take on the challenge of their adversaries in a fight for market, the challenge of consumers making their fastidious choices and the challenge of the new problems arising in the restructuring of our economic set-up. An ill-managed enterprise incapable of winning a competition deprives itself of life, which naturally brings its leaders before a most relentless test. A study of "Sun Zi" could be a boon to the prosperity of a business.

IV

The immortal military masterpiece that is "Sun Zi" contains a whole treasurehouse of ideas and principles of management which would be of service to business management. In our opinion, the cream of the work consists in three of its concepts which are of universal significance: 1. the concept of " 'Dao'

('The Right Way') as the top priority of the 'Five Key Factors' and the 'Seven Comparisons' "; 2. the axiom: "Know the enemy and know yourself, and you can fight a hundred battles with no danger of defeat;" and 3. the idea of winning a victory by "modifying one's tactics in accordance with the changes in enemy conditions". A discussion of these three concepts would outline the book of "Sun Zi" as a whole.

(1) " 'Dao' ('The Right Way') as the top priority of the 'Five Key Factors' and the 'Seven Comparisons' ". The book of "Sun Zi" opens with pointing out the importance of studying problems of warfare and turns immediately to the discussion of the need for studying the "Five Key Factors" and making seven "comparisons", both of which together constitute the key to the understanding of the classic. Sun Wu holds that "he who knows them (the Five Key Factors: 'Dao' ('The Righy Way'), Heavenly timeliness, Ground, Command and Institutions) will be victorious; he who does not will fail", that the seven comparisons will always allow one to forecast the outcome of a war: "which of the two sovereigns is the representative of 'the Right Way'? Which of the two commanders has greater ability? Which side has the advantages of heavenly timeliness and terrain? Which side is capable of enforcing regulations and orders more rigorously? Which troops are the stronger? Whose officers and men are better trained? And which army knows the greater strictness and impartiality in administering rewards and punishments?" Sun Wu also points out that studying the "Five Key Factors" and making the seven "comparisons" is the top concern, for "war is a matter of primary importance to the state" and "It brings life or death and leads to survival or ruin." All this represents a highly condensed generalization of Sun Wu's art of war and the focus of the might of the ancient treatise "Sun Zi". What is most noteworthy is that here Sun Wu puts "Dao" ("The Right Way") above everything else—an exceedingly brilliant idea which means that a just cause enjoys abundant support while an unjust cause finds little support, and the outcome of a war depends mainly on whether the people welcome the political line and the policies of a given ruler. It is this universally true idea of "Sun Zi" that makes the ancient military treatise radiate with the light of naive historical materialism. In business management, the same questions are to be

taken into consideration. Here, the term "Dao" may be interpreted as the basic principles of a business and the guidelines and objectives of its operation. The odds are that a business will be successful once it is on the right track in all these things and so there is agreement among its managers and employees, and they take concerted actions.

(2) "Know the enemy and know yourself, and you can fight a hundred battles with no danger of defeat". This statement is quoted from the classic's Chapter 3, "The Strategy of Attack". Also in Chapter 10, "Terrain", it is stated: "Know the enemy and know yourself, and you can always win, with no danger of defeat. Know the Heaven and know the Ground, and your victory is sure to be complete." Here, the emphasis is put on "knowing"—a truly materialist proposition reflecting the naive materialist thought contained in the treatise. Indeed, one simply cannot expect to win a war or to achieve success in a business, knowing neither oneself nor the adversary or knowing only one of the two. As Mao Zedong pointed out, "... Sun Wu Tzu's axiom, 'Know the enemy and know yourself, and you can fight a hundred battles with no dangers of defeat,' remains a scientific truth." ("Selected Works of Mao Tze-tung", Eng. ed., FLP, Peking, 1965, Vol. II, p. 164) He also said, "There is a saying in the book of Sun Wu Tzu, the great military scientist of ancient China, 'Know the enemy and know yourself, and you can fight a hundred battles with no danger of defeat', which refers both to the stage of learning and to the stage of application, both to knowing the laws of the development of objective reality and to deciding on our own action in accordance with these laws in order to overcome the enemy facing us. We should not take this saying lightly." ("Selected Works of Mao Tse-tung", Eng. ed., FLP, Peking, 1964, Vol, I, p. 190) Yes, the famous axiom of Sun Wu's, which might sound so as to awaken the deaf, has contributed to the success of so many causes since the ancient times and inspired so many people with lofty ideals in making their accomplishments, and so many entrepreneurs take this ancient saying as the motto for their managerial work.

(3) Win victory by modifying your tactics in accordance with the changes in enemy conditions. This saying of Sun Wu's reflects views of naive dialectics. It is found in Chapter 6, "The

Void and the Solid"; "... as water shapes its course in accordance with the ground, so an army forges its victory in accordance with the enemy conditions. Therefore, there are no constant patterns of war, just as water has no constant shape. He who can win victory by modifying his tactics in accordance with the changes in enemy conditions is considered divine." Such dialectical views of things are felt throughout the book of "Sun Zi" from cover to cover. The author always expresses his views by using concepts of unity of opposites such as motion and motionlessness, advantages and disadvantages, the regular and the irregular, the void and the solid, life and death, the devious and the direct, gains and losses, offensive and defensive, order and disorder, bravery and cowardice, the strong and the weak, and so on and so forth. Sun Wu discusses his principles of employing troops, saying that "those who know them will be victorious," while the art of winning a victory is "beyond any formulation beforehand". (See "Sun Zi", ch. 1, "Reckoning") By saying so he stresses the need for winning a victory by way of studying the changing conditions of the enemy. In Chapter 5 of the treatise, "Momentum", the strategist makes a statement brilliant with ideas of dialectical development: "... combined in various ways, the regular and the irregular produce so many manoeuvres that one can never know them all". "For the regular and the irregular elements change into each other in a cycle that neither begins nor ends like a ring. So who can possibly find the end of it?" In the light of the related statements of the author and the ideological dimension of the book as a whole, we learn that the endless cycle Sun Wu refers to is that of change, that of development, that of spiral ascension —a quite valuable concept of naive dialectics. Quite a few strategic and tactical principles of "Sun Zi" can be said to be derived from the basic tenet of winning a victory by reacting correctly to the changing conditions of the enemy, for it stresses "change", recognizing that things are changing and developing, and gives priority to dynamic management which means devising one's schemes for employing troops in a battle in accordance with the changes on the enemy's side. Business management is, like warfare, full of conflicts and contradictions. It is also of a dynamic nature; its guidelines and plans also involve problems of how to win a victory by reacting correctly to the changing conditions of the "enemy", (in this case, competitors). This is one of the basic principles vital for business management which knows no fixed ways just like the management of military affairs.

The limitations of the age and the class status by which Sun Wu was conditioned gave rise to some idealistic views in the treatise. For instance, the author attributes the occurrence and the prevention of war to the whims of a commander instead of the struggle of classes. Quite a few of his views of the role of soldiers are wrong. He calls for "making the soldiers ignorant in eyes as well as in ears". (See "Sun Zi", ch. 11, "The Nine Varieties of Battleground") And he parallels the direction of troops with "driving flocks of sheep here and there so that they know not where." (Ibid.) Some biased views on problems of strategy and tactics are found in the treatise. The role of strategic defense, for one, has not been emphasized to a proper degree.

A monumental military work, "Sun Zi" was born as a historical summary of experience, its great significance has been affirmed in the process of historical development, and it will surely be enriched by the realities of today. The ancient can be made to serve the present, the military—to serve civilian purposes, just as an old Chinese saying puts it, "Stones from other hills may serve to polish the jade of this one". The quintessence of "Sun Zi" is surely of good service to business management and administration.

It would have been a matter of course for us Chinese to make use of the ancient treatise in our business management which still remains relatively backward in China. In the past, however, research in this field was neglected.

It was impossible to advocate scientific management itself in the days before the downfall of the "leftist" "Gang of Four" in 1976 when scientific management was labelled as "revisionist, capitalist stuff" and its advocaters would have been declared "restorationists", to say nothing of studying problems of how to apply the thought of "Sun Zi" to management. It was only after the Third Plenum of the 11th National Congress of the Communist Party of China held in 1978 when the Party decided to shift its stress of work to the modernization of the country that some people began to study ways to apply part of the scientific concepts and ideas of "Sun Zi" to business management to serve the needs of China's modernization drive. Nevertheless, we are still lagging behind in this respect both theoretically and in practice.

The application of the thought of "Sun Zi" to business management was initiated by the Japanese entrepreneurs and scientists of management. The Japanese display a great zeal in studying this problem. As is reported by the newspaper "Wen Wei Po" in Hongkong, "In Japan, not only those engaged in military and defence studies consider 'Sun Zi' as their obligatory course, but also baseballists have quotations from 'Sun Zi' on their lips. A Japanese entrepreneur called Takeo Ohashi wrote a book entitled 'Management by Art of War' in which he taught how to do business in this way." It is said that his company enhanced its efficiency of work remarkably and promoted its business rapidly after adopting the theories of "Sun Zi". The newspaper also quoted Takeo Ohashi as saying, "This way of business management is even more rational and efficient than that in the United States." Mr. Mulayama, a Japanese expert working with China's Japanese language magazine *"Ginmin Chiugogu"* ("People's China"), said that the managers of the medium-sized and small enterprises in Japan put special emphasis on the study of Chinese classical thoughts, particularly the study of the ancient treatise "Sun Zi". In order to strengthen its management and administration, a big Japanese corporation organized one-month courses for leaders at middle level and above to study "Sun Zi" as their chief subject. Twelve such courses in a year covered all who were required to attend them. The corporation demanded that the trainees study the management of today and the supposed tactics for the development of their enterprises in the light of the ancient Chinese military work "Sun Zi". Mr. Mulayama also told us that in order to keep their business alive and growing, the Japanese entrepreneurs have two "pillars", or "wheels", at their disposal: modern American management theory used in times of boom and classical Chinese thought, the thought contained in "Sun Zi" in particular, used in times of depression. Perhaps the penetrating views on devising strategic plans and tactics for counteraction are, as Mr. Mulayama has confirmed, what is of particular significance for the survival of the Japanese business in depression. As a matter of fact, the scientific ideas of "Sun Zi" are equally useful to a business both in boom and in depression. A Japanese book entitled "How to Be Leader of a Business", written by Kuniyoshi Ulape, elaborates on the statement of "Sun Zi"—"By command are meant the general's qualities of wisdom, good faith, humanity, courage and strictness". (See "Sun Zi", ch. 1, "Reckoning") The author holds that a leader should live up to the five qualities of a commander as is required by Sun Wu and that "they are still applicable today, two millennia and more beyond." Some American scholars wrote books in praise of the management ideas contained in "Sun Zi". And there is no lack of people pursuing the study in this field in Hongkong and Taiwan.

Since the foreigners are earnest in studying "Sun Zi", one of the gems in the wonderful legacy of Chinese culture, we Chinese should all the more treasure it and strive to extract what is best in it to serve our present needs.

This book of ours, " 'Sun Wu's Art of War' and the Art of Business Management", represents a first attempt to explore ways of growing the marvelous flower of "Sun Zi" on the green fields of the Chinese-style business management together with the comrades who are keen on research work in this connection.

V

The military treatise "Sun Zi" is rich in concepts, principles and methods of work more or less applicable in business management and administration. This book of ours will deal with their application to the real process of production managment and business operation. As we see it, the process of production management and business operation is one of developments in the unity of opposites, one that compromises the need for satisfying social demands and the need for satisfying the demands of the business itself for its survival and growth. Business management is a process of satisfying both these demands through effective division of labour and cooperation inside the enterprise. The process of production management and business operation may be divided into three stages:

The stage of decision-making. This is the stage in which to learn about, analyze and judge the demands of the society and the market for material production, to study the problems to be solved by the enterprise in its endeavour to meet the needs of the society and to find out what needs of the enterprise itself are to be satisfied and to what a degree while achieving the goal of meeting the needs of the society. And the strategic, tactical and executive plans are made in the light of the studies mentioned above.

The stage of production management. This is the stage in which to make investments and turn out products. Here the manager has to do a good job of organizing various resources available (manpower, materials, finance, technology, information, etc.) for the labourers to use so that a maximum of good economic results is achieved with a minimum of investment of the resources.

The stage of sales promotion. This is the stage in which to put the products into circulation by means of sales and managment so that they are tested on the market and judged in competition, their value and use value are realized, and wealth is added for the state and profit is gained for the enterprise.

This book of ours, " 'Sun Wu's Art of War' and the Art of Business Management", basing itself on these three stages of the process of production management and business operation, deals with ways of making use of the concepts, principles and methods as revealed in "Sun Zi" to help improve business decision-making, production management and sales promotion, giving priority to the problems of business strategy and tactics and organizational administration. Dealing with business decision-making, we will, above all, study how to apply Sun Wu's concepts of "reckoning" and "scheming" to business planning. Studying production management, we will emphasize ways to apply Sun Wu's principles of organizing, directing and "commanding many." In the discussion of sales promotion, Sun Wu's strategy of counteraction will be drawn upon to find ways to promote sales. And the indispensable qualities of a "commander" in business management will also be dealt with in this book. Thus, the book is organized like this:

1. Reckoning and scheming before a battle— key to business decision-making;

2. To make yourself invincible before fighting a battle, and

organize a proper administration of the collective— things at the core of production management;

3. Ingenuity in sales promotion—a salient point in the competition for market;

4. "Five Virtues" required of a commander—essentials for a business leader.

Chapter 1
Reckoning and Scheming Before a Battle
—Key to Business Decision-Making

Reckoning and scheming come first in directing military operations. First work out your plans, and then dispatch your troops beyond the border.

When you just take over the management of an enterprise or you intend to bring a new look into the enterprise you are responsible for, you know there is very much to be done. But what is the first and foremost thing to be considered and to put your hand to? Reckoning and scheming. Making plans to ensure your victory. Scheming means making a plan for action, working out business strategy and business tactics.

By strategy we mean the plans and tactics for directing the development of the overall situation of war, or analogically the tactics of decisive significance for any situation as a whole. As regards the management and administration of an enterprise, business strategy includes the major policies of an enterprise as a whole: for example, those concerning the patterns of its products, the market of the products, and sales tactics.

In China, it was not until after the Third Plenum of the Eleventh National Congress of the Communist Party of China that the question of business strategy of the enterprise was raised. The state has introduced a policy for the predominence of a planned economy while making market regulation subsidiary, recognizing the enterprise as a relatively independent entity of commodity production and business operation. As a result, the enterprise has been given more decision-making power in its operation and has been switched from production-oriented management to production-and-operation-oriented management, from management aimed at the increase of output value to management put on the track of enhancing economic results.

This switch of the pattern of business management and the objectives of production calls for a sober strategic mind of the business leader who should have a good grasp of the "ways" of management in the ever-changing reality. The "ways" of management of a socialist enterprise in China can be summed up like this:

Guideline—"Four Cardinal Principles"; (i.e. adherence to the socialist road, to the people's democratic dictatorship, to the leadership of the Party, and to Marxism-Leninism-Mao Zedong Thought.)

Goal—to meet the material and cultural needs of the people;

Basis for growth—the enhancement of economic results;

Focus of attention—the development of the enterprise in the future;

Things to strive for—reform and innovation.

Reckoning and scheming, or making plans, should come first in the operation of a business, just as in military affairs. An enterprise should work out its own strategy for operation meaning a correct policy of operation, an advanced and rational objective of operation and a feasible operational plan.

The policy of operation means the principles of operational activities and those for solving various questions arising in operation. A case in point is the principle set by some competing enterprises—to win a competition with new products, fine quality, cheaper price, good service and good faith in fulfilling contracts. The objective of operation is what an enterprise strives for in a given period of time, with fixed numerical standands to check on and assess by. The operational plan meaning the tactical choices and procedural arrangements to be made for the realization of the objective of operation, includes tactical plans and executive plans. The former serves the interests of strategic aims, directing the development of the enterprise and formulating its objectives, while the latter means plans of action for attaining these objectives. The objective and the plan always go together, for an objective without a plan of action will remain a mere ideal, and a plan without a definite objective will be utterly worthless.

The process of deciding on a policy of operation, an objective of operation and an operational plan is none other than one of devising strategy and schemes which is the responsibility of a business leader.

1. Reckon Before a Battle;
Know the Enemy and Know Yourself

(A) Correct Reckoning of the Conditions of the Enemy and Those of Yourself.

In " 'Sun Zi' with Annotations by Eleven Scholars", Du Mu points out: "Scheming means reckoning." To decide on a scheme, to carry out a tactical plan, one must resort to reckoning, reckoning by means of numbers. The outcome of a battle involves numerical reckoning of advantages and disadvantages, which is of vital importance to military manoeuvres. Therefore, one who directs a war ought to know all factors affecting its outcome. In "Sun Zi", Chapter 3, "The Strategy of Attack", it is stated: "Know the enemy and know yourself, and you can fight a hundred battles with no danger of defeat. When you do not know the enemy but know yourself, you will stand an even chance of winning. If you know neither your enemy nor yourself, danger will keep you company in every battle." Thus, Sun Wu demonstrates in a simple and unequivocable language the importance of knowing both the enemy and oneself for those who direct a war and its connection with the war's outcome, revealing the law governing warfare that a correct decision always comes with a proper knowledge of conditions. And this law governing warfare, followed by military leaders at home and abroad since ancient times, is now taken as a strategic principle in political, economic and other fields. Indeed, the saying "Know the enemy and know yourself, and you can fight a hundred battles with no danger of defeat" has now become one of the basic concepts of many entrepreneurs in making decisions and the maxim for guiding their activities in production and operation.

What is meant by "the enemy", and what is by "oneself" in business management? By "the enemy" here we mean all factors relating to and surrounding an operating business and the responses from all sides to the information given out by that business. The former may include data on the competitors and competition-related information about the political and economic situation, the market and channels of supply in the countries and areas concerned. The latter may include responses to an advertisement or sales activities. By "oneself" here we mean, above all, the strength of an enterprise itself and the information of all kinds it brings forth in making decisions and arranging production processes. By the strength of an enterprise is meant, among other things, the advantages and shortcomings of its products, their service life and market share, the total amount of the resources in the possession of the enterprise and those accessible to it, and the proficiency of its management, operation and organization. In modern management, to know the adversary and oneself would mean to get external and internal information. To know the adversary is to get the external information needed by the enterprise, and to know oneself is to know and keep under control the internal information stream. In the information system of business management, external information consists of two kinds of information running in opposite directions: One is intelligence data coming into an enterprise from its operational surroundings in an information stream and having long-term significance for fixing its objectives of operation and making its operational plans. The other is communications information, i.e., the information flowing out of the enterprise to its operational surroundings in the form of advertisement, sales activities, etc. Although this kind of information is given out by the enterprise in a controlled way, the enterprise must find out how people respond to it, or, in other words, get hold of the feedback information, in order to work out its strategy, objectives and plans of operation. And this is an essential part of the efforts to know the adversary. The stream of information is the process in which the incoming intelligence data converge with the information arising inside the enterprise and flow together to the managers. Such a stream of information runs not only vertically from the managers to the managed, from the higher-ups to the subordinates, but also horizontally, from one department to another and from one section to another. To keep the stream of information inside the enterprise under control is an essential part of the efforts to "know yourself."

Discussing how to elaborate military plans, Mao Zedong

pointed out: "A commander's correct dispositions stem from his correct decisions, his correct decisions stem from his correct judgements, and his correct judgements stem from a thorough and necessary reconnaissance and from pondering on and piecing together the data of various kinds gathered through reconnaissance. He applies all possible and necessary methods of reconnaissance, and ponders on the information gathered about the enemy's situation, discarding the dross and selecting the essential, eliminating the false and retaining the true, proceeding from one thing to another and from the outside to the inside; then he takes the conditions on his own side into account, and makes a comparative study of both sides and their interrelations, thereby forming his judgement, making up his mind and working out his plans." ("Selected Works of Mao Tse-tung", Eng. ed., FLP, Peking, 1964, Vol. 1, p. 188) Here, Mao Zedong made a penetrating analysis of the cognition involved in working out a military plan and showed two basic principles guiding the work: "Know the enemy and know yourself" and "Win victory by modifying your tactics in accordance with the changes in the enemy conditions." These, of course, are equally applicable in working out the guidelines and plans for business operation, which calls for knowledge of the conditions of the adversary and those of your own and careful reckoning before an action is taken. Only with the details of the situation in mind can you work out your correct guidelines and plans.

From the above-stated one can see that "the enemy" or "oneself" is to be specified in different ways, depending on categories of the subjects under discussion and conditions things are subject to. With business management of an enterprise working out its operational plans, the enterprise represents the subject ("oneself"), while the outside environment—the object ("the enemy"). In the contest with your competitor, you represent "oneself", while the adversary—"the enemy". So far as the handling of relations with people is concerned, the manager becomes the subject ("oneself"), whereas his leaders, subordinates and people at his own level are all objects ("the enemy"). While working out operational plans, objectives for operation and production plans, you are required to have a good grasp of the concepts "the enemy" and "oneself" according to the specific categories of

23

things and specific situations you are dealing with under given conditions. Only in this way can you prevent one-sidedness in your understanding. Since our book explores the links between the ancient military treatise "Sun Zi" and business management in the light of the process of management, the phrase "to know the enemy and know yourself" mentioned in Chapter 1 means, first of all, to get information of all kinds concerning business operation from both inside and outside the enterprise. As to the concepts of "the enemy" and "oneself" with regard to the relations between men, we will deal with them in the following chapters.

For the leading body of an enterprise, knowing "the enemy" and itself serves the purpose of making correct decisions. One of the methods of making a decision and ways of carrying it out, which the treatise "Sun Zi" often refers to is to try one's best to translate the conditions known of the enemy and oneself into countable numbers and then make analysis of them and compare those of the two sides. Chapter 4 of "Sun Zi", "Position", points out: "In military affairs there are five essentials to be taken into consideration: first, measurements; second, quantities and capacities; third, numbers; fourth, balance of power; and fifth, chances of victory. Measurements of space and terrain are decided by the ground; quantities and capacities by the measurements, numbers of troops by the quantities and capacities, balance of power by the numbers of troops, and chances of victory by the balance of power." In other military treatises, this "method of five essentials" is known as "Calculate and Judge". In "Sun Zi," the chief factors determining or affecting the outcome of a war are summarized as "five key factors" (called by the later generations as "top priorities of military affairs"), and from them are derived "seven comparisons." Chapter 1 of "Sun Zi", "Reckoning", states: "... it is imperative to base one's judgement of the situation of war on the five key factors and compare the conditions of the warring sides, whereby to explore the circumstances leading to victory or defeat," and so "forecast which side will win and which lose." The same chapter states that the "five key factors" are "first, 'Dao' ('The Right Way'); second, heavenly timeliness; third, ground; fourth, command; and fifth, institutions"; and defines the seven "comparisons" as: "Which of the two sovereigns is the representative of 'the Right Way'? Which of the two commanders has greater ability? Which side has the advantages of heavenly timeliness and ground? Which side is capable of enforcing regulations and orders more rigorously? Which troops are the stronger? Whose officers and men are better trained? And which army knows the greater strictness and impartiality in administering rewards and punishments?"

In determining a business policy, the various conditions determining or affecting the competitiveness of an enterprise can usually be translated into some countable numbers. The specific conceptional and psychological factors pertinent to one of the sides concerned can also be weighed and compared by the decision-makers by means of specific terminology and corresponding criteria of measurement. A comparative study in the form of a table would illustrate how a business manager might draw upon teachings of "Sun Zi" about the "five key factors" and the "seven comparisons" in making his decisions.

Table One
"Five Key Factors" as Interpreted for Warfare and Business Management Respectively

	In Warfare	**In Business Management**
"Dao" (The Right Way)	1. Fine political conditions; "Benevolence and Righteousness"—foundation of a victory in warfare. 2. Decrees and regulations; laws concerning warfare; ingenuity in varying tactics.	1. The political line, guidelines and policies of the state; the role of law in business management. 2. A correct guiding principle of operation. 3. Concepts and methods of management in keeping with economic laws and laws of nature.
Heavenly timeliness	Time and weather: Day or night; rain or shine; alteration of four seasons; etc.	Political and economic position of the country or the locality; climatic conditions.

Ground	Geographical conditions —whether the field of battle is far or near, difficult or easy of access, broad or narrow, favourable for attack and defence, for advance and retreat, or not.	Geographical location of the enterprise and the resultant amount of accessible resources (manpower and materials); regions or countries the enterprise's products go to; the distance to these regions or countries and communication means; the presence or absence of competitors, ux numbers and competitive power.
Command	"Five Virtues" required of a commander: Wisdom: gift for strategic decisions; resourcefulness. Good Faith: to be trust-worthy in meting out rewards and punishment. Humanity: concern and love for soldiers. Courage: to be fearless and resolute in action. Strictness: to be strict in enforcing military discipline.	"Five Virtues" desirable in a business manager: Wisdom: resourcefulness and talents; professional proficiency, gifts for thinking, prediction, judgement and accommodation. Good faith: never to break one's word; to put full faith in the subordinates. Humanity: concern and love for the subordinates, making allowance for them. Courage: to be resolute in handling things, to make decisions and take actions in time, to be keen on reform and innovation.
Institutions	Rigorous implementation of the institutions and regulations of the army concerning the size and structure of the army, requirements for it, definition of duties incumbent on each post, logistics system, etc.	Rigorous implementation of rules and regulations concerning the organizational structure of the enterprise, requirements for accommodation, disposition of personnel, definition of responsibility and power, etc.

**Seven "Comparisons" as Applied to Warfare and
Business Management Respectively**

In Warefare	In Business Management
Which of the two sovereigns effects an enlightened rule?	Which of the enterprises concerned has a wiser decision-making body of managers?
Which of the two commanders is more talented, more qualified in terms of wisdom, good faith, humanity, courage and strictness?	Which of the competing enterprises has more qualified leaders in terms of ability and political integrity?
Which of the warring sides is favoured by weather conditins and geographical advantages?	Which of the competing enterprises or their markets is more favoured by political and economic environment and geographical location?
Which of the two sides is capable of enforcing its decrees and regulations properly?	Which of the competing enterprises is more capable of enforcing its rules and regulations properly?
Which side possesses a more powerful military strength?	Which of the competing enterprises possesses greater power in terms of the quality of personnel, the quantities and qualities of resources including funds, manpower, materials, technology, information, etc.?
Which side has achieved a better training of its troops?	Which of the competing enterprises trains its personnel more effectively to make them more skilled and more qualified educationally and professionally?
Whose commander is strict and fair in meting out rewards and punishment?	Which of the competing enterprises is strict and fair in meting out rewards and punishment and thereby gets better results?

Many works on management point out that, working out a business strategy, a business manager finds it not so hard to conclude what objectives are to be set as to decide how to define these objectives. The method of reckoning as is stated above can be a guide to defining objectives of operation for a business manager. Objectives fixed by this method will be logically well-based and conforming to reality, and plans resulted from such reckoning will be well-calculated and realistic, because what this method stresses is to base one's objectives and plans on the knowledge of oneself and the adversary instead of the wishful thinking of a manager and to make comprehensive study, analysis and judgement of all the information available before deciding on a policy. In that case, the plans will surely be feasible and the objectives put forward can surely be realized.

(B) More Reckoning Beforehand to Ensure Better Chances of Winning.

In Chapter 1 of "Sun Zi", "Reckoning", it is stated: "Now if you estimate in the temple before a battle.* that victory will be yours, it is because you have secured all the favourable conditions and you make many calculations;** if you estimate that your victory will be most unlikely, it is because you have hardly all the favourable conditions and you make few calculations.*** With the necessary conditions and many calculations you can win; with few of them, you cannot, to say nothing of the case when they are absent. By examining this point I can foresee who is to win and who is to lose."

This statement of "Sun Zi" focuses on three questions of decision-making and scheming:

(1) More reckoning beforehand is needed. Careful, comprehensive, far-reaching consideration must be given to the actions to be taken before a strategic decision is made. Estimates must be made of what may crop up in a war, with both favourable and infavourable possibilities in view and various measures to deal with them in mind. This means that a war must be fought well-prepared, free from a wait-and-see approach and any belated actions or advices.

(2) More favourable conditions must be made available. By

---

*The ancient military leaders held some ceremony before a battle in the ancestral temple where they discussed plans and made calculations by means of some bamboo chips one *fen* (0.333 cm.) across and six *cun* (19.999 cm.) long.

**Literally, "... because you have secured many bamboo chips for calculation."

***Literally, "... because you have secured few bamboo chips for calculation."—*Trans.*

"securing many bamboo chips for calculation" Sun Wu means to secure as many conditions indispensable to victory as possible, to pit your superiority against the enemy's inferiority, to make a decision to fight a battle you are sure to win, to avoid staking everything on a single throw and acting from impulse.

(3) A sixty-percent chance of success is good reason for taking an action. One who excels at making decisions never makes one when he is one hundred percent sure of success. Decision-making is always accompanied by risks. Making a decision when everything is clear and ready is no decision-making at all, for anyone can easily do so. We should remember that to wait until each and every condition needed is ready often means to let the best chances slip through your fingers, that seeking "perfection" will leave one without a golden opportunity. "Sixty chips and more are many, and less than sixty chips are few," as an old Chinese saying goes. That means that when chances are sixty percent, one should make his decision and act with full confidence. In a sense, risks taken are proportional to the profit to be gained. Great risks will bring big profit when success is achieved. Profit is the reward for the risks taken. A decision made with no risks can never be a wise one, while taking risks without any "reckoning" beforehand is, of course, something least advisable.

The Loyang Tractor Plant producing tractors of the type "Dongfanghong 54" was confronted with the problems of whether to switch to other products and how to put an end to the passive position in which it had found itself when those tractors became dull of sales after the introduction of the system of contracted responsibility for production in agriculture. Some people in the plant favoured the production of the original tractors which they held would sell well again some day. Others were for a switch to 12-h.p. walking tractors, and still others—to 14-h.p. 4-wheeled small tractors which in their opinion were good for both ploughing and transportation. Those who were against held that tractors of these two types should not be put into production as they were already being turned out in some other plants in north China. After weighing the pros and cons and studying the conditions of the plant and those of others, the plant's managers reached the conclusion that chances of success for the two types were sixty percent and decided to put them into production. The decision proved correct, as the new products found ready market and brought back the initiative to the tractor plant.

2. Find out the Enemy Situation First, and Then Victory Will Be Yours

The ancients said, "To know the enemy situation is the foundation of war" and "Don't go into a war without knowing the enemy situation first." This is also true of business management. The information needed for fixing the operational objectives of an enterprise and determining the total amount and variety of the resources indispensable to attaining the objectives and that needed for working out the policies of managing the resources used, come for the most part from the outside, from intelligence data and the effective communications of the enterprise. Practice of business management has shown that the hardest thing for a business leader to do is to get hold of the appropriate information rather than to make decisions. Once the situation is made clear, making decisions is just a matter of course. Therefore, making decisions presupposes knowledge of "the enemy", i.e. the various factors in the world surrounding the business operation, which have an important bearing on the making of the operational policy of an enterprise and the realization of its goals. Thus the key to making a proper decision in business management lies in closely following the changes in quotations, keeping a close watch on what is going on with the market and the competitors, and trying in every way to get a clear picture of the surrounding world. Let us draw on some statements of "Sun Zi" that stresses learning about "the enemy" by means of scheming and spying for elaborating on three ways of doing so in business management.

(A) Keeping Close Watch over the Enemy—Method of Direct Observation.

To keep close watch over the enemy means to observe the movements of the enemy directly. Chapter 9 of "Sun Zi", "Marches", states: "Generally when you dispose your troops and observe the enemy, keep close to valleys on your march across mountains, encamp in high places commanding a broad view, and do not ascend to attack an enemy on a height. That is how to dispose troops in mountains." This means that the disposition of troops and judgement of the enemy's movements depend on a careful observation and study of the geographical positions and other conditions of both warring sides. To observe means to see for oneself.

Direct observation has long been resorted to in business decision-making. Take for instance: A manager goes to his shop to serve behind the counter; a factory director pays visit to the customers; the salesmen go about to make inquiries about the prevailing prices; such practices as to invite some customers and solicit their opinions, to sponsor sales exhibitions, to make inquiries through sending letters or by telephone are common. Direct observation can let you discover problems in time and bring about quick results. Examples: The once popular men's shirt with pointed-ended collar was mass produced by the Haiyan shirt factory of Zhejiang Province after its agents sent to a Shanghai clothing store to serve behind the counter learned from the talks of some young people how they took interest in that sort of shirts. The Taojiang County plastics products factory in Hunan Province, a small factory of 140-odd workers, which turned out engineering plastic products before 1979, found no market for them in the recent years. The overstock caused arrears of the workers' wages. In January 1981, the factory organized five market investigation groups under its director and vice-directors. They went round a dozen provinces and cities to find out how things stood with the demand for and supply of plastic products on the urban and rural markets, and organized some consignment-sale and trial-selling points for the factory's products in Wuhan, Zhengzhou, Changsha and Zhuzhou to know the opinions of the customers. Quite a few of them told the investigators that small fittings made of plastics are nowhere to be bought as the plastics factories preferred the production of large-size products to that of small ones. The information acquired through direct observation during visits and trial-selling prompted the leaders of the factory to make the decision of "developing the small products and winning market by making good omissions and deficiencies," and to call for "attention to the odds-and-ends and patient, scrupulous service." As a result, the factory soon found its business brisking up. Take four of its small products: the ring, handle, top and string of the umbrella. One set of them brought a total profit of only five *fen* (0.05 *yuan*), but "many a little makes a mickle"—two hundred thousand sets of them produced in 1981, valued at over ten thousand yuan and sold to the last piece, brought a profit of over two thousand yuan. The profit gained by the factory in the first two quarters of 1982 alone amounted to over 44 thousand yuan. The Kinfeng clothing factory in Shanghai discovered through investigation of the clothing patterns of the city residents by its observation posts that many workers have their work clothes remade. So the factory decided to make these clothes a "latest fashion". More than 40 kinds of work clothes suitable for various types of work were designed and produced and were warmly received by the public.

By "keeping close watch over the enemy" one can not only "seize the target" directly, but also see the essence of things behind phenomena and decide on a strategy through reasoning. Chapter 9 of "Sun Zi", "Marches," states: "When the enemy is in close proximity yet keeps quiet, he is counting on a hardly accessible position. When he is far yet challenges to battle he is waiting for your advance. When he stays where there is easy access, it must be to his advantage. Trees which are seen moving show that the enemy is coming. Obstacles scattered in profusion among the tall grass mean that the enemy wants to mislead you. Birds shooting upwards suggest that there must be ambush beneath...." This shows that while "keeping close watch over the enemy" one can find out what is going on with "the enemy" by reasoning logically about causes and effects.

The Henan opera "General Hua Mulan" gives an episode about how the woman general, upon hearing the startling of birds at night while making her rounds of the camps, decided that the Turkis were going to make a surprise attack and scored a great victory by first emptying out her camps and laying her troops in ambush. This is just a case of making a decision to win by means of analysis of causes and effects after observing the enemy. The theoretical basis for doing so lies in the very statement of "Sun Zi": "Trees which are seen moving show that the enemy is coming.... Birds shooting upwards suggest that there must be ambush beneath."

There is no lack of instances of success in business operation resulting from "observing the enemy" and reasoning about the clues discovered to "the enemy's" situation. The Zhanghua woolen mill in Shanghai discovered in 1981 in its investigation of the market that people rushed to buy the valitin originally intended for export, in spite of the fact that valitin, once popular in China in the 1950s, had disappeared from the domestic market about twenty years before. An idea dawned on the leaders of the mill, and its first 80 thousand metres of valitin appeared on the market in February 1982 and were sold out instantly.

Besides finding out the enemy's situation through direct observation, one can also watch one's time and act after a long-time observation. In 1982, at the Thomas Cup badminton tournament, the game of China's Han Jian versus Indonesia's Liem Swie King was to be a decisive one. First the opponents each won a set. Han Jian led 14-9 in the third set, and Liem hit back strongly to level at 14-14. There additional points were to be vied for. Han met the attack with composure and won two points successively. The third and the last point would be decisive. After a little recollection, Han served the shuttlecock to the left of the other side, to which Liem responded with a lift to sent the shuttlecock just over the net. Han lunged for a drop shot to Liem's astonishment, and the blitz brought him victory. This crucial plunge of Han's was by no means accidental. Han Jian said, "I discovered through years of observation that Liem invariably responded to that way of my attack with a lift to send the shuttlecock just over the net. In this game I had plunged like this only once, so that he wouldn't take notice of it. This trick of mine I reserved for the final stroke." A case of "Know the enemy and know yourself and you can fight a hundred battles with no danger of defeat"! Kartono, another Indonesian star shuttler, said with admiration after the game, "Marvellous was Han Jian's play today!"

Han Jian's method of observing the enemy many years for "a crucial plunge" to subdue him could be of considerable value to business decision-making. For instance the energy crisis presented a threat to world automobile industry in general, but the Japanese automakers who had always emphasized the development of fuel-saving cars saw in it a chance for success. Just as U.S. President J. Carter proposed protection of resources, and the U.S. government drew up an act for returning tax payment to the owners of fuel-efficient cars, and began to implement it, the Japanese automakers lost no time in flooding the American automobile market with such cars, getting the Ford Moto Company into a bad fix by this "crucial plunge".

(B) Manoeuvring the Enemy—Method of Guiding the Enemy into the Desired Position.

Chapter 5 of "Sun Zi", "Momentum", states: "... one who excels at manoeuvring the enemy puts up a false front, and the enemy will surely be led by it." To manoeuvre the enemy means to get the concealed or inconspicuous conditions of the enemy revealed in every way, or to guide the enemy into the desired position. Many ways of manoeuvring the enemy are given in the ancient treatise "Sun Zi", and here we would like to offer a view of those of them which may be of some use for business management.

(1) "Give him a stir"—Method of reconnaissance by firing. In Chapter 6 of "Sun Zi", "The Void and the Solid," it is stated: "Give him a stir, and you will know what rules his movements." This is just what is meant today by "reconnaissance by firing." A small detachment sneaking toward the enemy's position makes a surprise attack by opening fire with a few rifles, which induces the enemy soldiers in their pillboxes, open or secret, to shoot back in a hurry, revealing the location of their firing points. Then the scouts put these on the map for the reference of the decision-makers.

This "method of reconnaissance by firing" can be useful for finding out what is beyond direct observation. For instance, an enterprise wants to know the suitability of developing a product or a service inside the country or in the given locality, which are already available and even popular on the market abroad. The answer lies, among other things, in the "method of reconnaissance by firing"—Give it a stir!

Early in 1981, the Yunnan Chemical Engineering Fittings Plant, having learned that the Shanghai Non-Ferrous Metal Welding Plant was very popular and aluminum products brought big profits in other provinces, intended to start its non-ferrous metal welding services in Yunnan. To find out whether this will be as "popular" as in Shanghai, the plant resorted to "reconnaissance by firing", advertising for business discussions concerning non-ferrous metal welding and manufacturing. Very soon the advertisement received warm responses from a lot of enterprises and supply and marketing cooperatives, a workshop of non-ferrous metal welding was established at the plant, and its business started. The 22-member workshop yielded a net profit of 70 thousand yuan in 1980 and 100 thousand in 1981.

This method can also be desirable for the trial-production and trial-selling of new products. One can first turn out a batch of a given new product for sale in other cities and provinces or even abroad, send it to the market at fixed points, collect the customers' opinions about its quality, specifications and pricing, speculate on the purchasing will of the public, and then decide whether his enterprise is going to produce it in batches and how much of it is to be produced.

(2) "Make displays to entice him"—Method of reconnaissance by luring and inducing through display.

Chapter 6 of "Sun Zi", "The Void and the Solid", states: "Make displays to entice him and you will know what positions of the enemy are vulnerable and what ones not." It is obvious that this display is a false move by which to find out the actual situation of the enemy and to ascertain where the enemy is more vulnerable. In warfare, being stronger than the enemy, you may display yourself as being weak so as to lure the enemy to where you want him to go, while, being weaker than the enemy, you may display yourself as being strong so as to make the enemy flee with fear. Your display can direct the enemy's movements. In business, you may likewise display yourself, your real self, to attract the customers, get the response of the market and finally gain your profit. This is what we call the method of luring and inducing through display to "know the enemy".

Business knows luring and inducing through display as a common practice. The Shanghai No. 1 Department Store replenished its stock with a batch of cut glass drinking vessels in the summer of 1982. One set of them consisted of six long-stemmed glasses which were beautifully designed and of high quality. At first, they received a cold response from the public, just a few sets of them being sold in a whole day. Then some young shop assistants hit upon a good idea. They poured some water in the glasses and mixed a few drops of red ink in it, so that the glasses sparkled attractively as if with grape wine. Such a display drew the customers' attention, and the sale soared to 30-40 sets a day.

The advantage of display is that it allows the customers to know at a glance the quality of a product or a service, and it always brings instant market response. The Shanghai fashion show team organized in 1980 was a team for displaying fashionable dresses. In dresses of various designs, its girl members danced with sandalwood fans to the accompaniment of the violin concerto "Liang Shanbo and Zhu Yingtai", and the boy members walked, turned, lifted hands and legs, posed and changed their positions to show the spectators the original Chinese tailoring skills. Customers and traders from other places of the country commented that these dresses seemed much more beautiful on the mannequins than they did on display in the shopwindows. The fashion show brought fame to Shanghai's fashionable dresses on the domestic market and aroused great interest in the trade delegations of many foreign countries, opening a new way for Chinese clothing to enter the world market. On Shanghai's fashion show of 1982, the Soviet trade delegation made a deal of purchasing 15 million U.S. dollars' worth of fashionable dresses of 51 designs. At the trade talks held in Shanghai in 1983, a fashion show amazed and excited the foreign businessmen with one-hundred-odd patterns of clothing which were in vogue abroad. An American businessman asked to place his orders at once. When told that this was just a show, he expressed his wish to buy the samples the mannequins had put on themselves. Obviously, it is much more effective a way of striking a bargain to show the customers the product or service itself first than to solicit business without displaying the goods. More examples of offering commodities or services through direct display are: toys performing on the counter, printed sheets spread or hung for display, exhibitions of manufactured goods, TV commercials, a kitchen knife seller "chopping" ironware with it, a watermelon seller splitting one for all to see, and so on and so forth.

There are, however, some products and services which cannot show their worth on their own. Only when they are related to other products or services can they display their functions and qualities properly. That is where indirect display comes in, display with the help of some media. In 1982, the Chinese paper "Economic Information" carried an interesting story entitled "Why shoes are shined free?" It told of a young man selling a new liquid shoe polish produced by the Chongqing factory of chemicals for daily use. Beside a standing paper sign reading: "First shine, then buy!" he cried his wares in this way: "Shine your shoes free, and decide if you'll buy the polish!" When a curious passer-by stretched out his foot, the salesman put a little of that liquid on his leather shoe, rubbed it with a piece of cotton flannel, and the shoe shone as bright as could be. Then a girl, his partner, came forward and, pointing at the glistening shoe, set off her "advertising", which caused a rush to buy the new polish. The author of the story commented, "If the salespeople had just put the liquid polish on the ground and kept silence, the passers-by would have just looked at it a little while and hesitated to buy it, for they would have had a question mark in their minds as to the quality of the new product. The experiment they made on the spot displaying the quality of their shoe polish with the help of the shoe of a passer-by turned the question mark in the minds of the onlookers into an exclamation mark—"It's a good thing!" A certain radio equipment factory in Shanghai advertised its rectifiers on television by informing the TV watchers that they are being used in the earth satellites, warships and best TV sets of the country instead of simply stating the function and the quality of the rectifiers themselves. Thus, the customers sensed the fineness of the quality of the factory's rectifiers through association with the technological standards for earth satellites, warships and best TV sets. And this was exactly what the advertisement was for.

(3) "Probe him with a skirmish"—Method of reconnaissance by coming to grips with the enemy.

In Chapter 6 of "Sun Zi", "The Void and the Solid", it is stated: "Probe him with a skirmish and you will know where his forces are strong and where weak." This is a method of reconnaissance by coming to grips with the enemy.

Both reconnaissance by coming to grips with the enemy and reconnaissance by firing are ways of finding out the enemy's real situation. The former is an open contest of strength in a direct confrontation of the opponents and brings, as a rule, information of overall importance, while the latter is but a minor engagement, a shock attack by a small detachment, which, in a sense, serves only tactical purposes and therefore brings information far more limited in its depth and breadth than that the former does. There is no lack of instances of reconnaissance by coming to grips with the enemy in the history of war.

According to "Shuo Yuan," ("A Collection of Commentaries", a Confucian work by Liu Kiang who lived in the Western Han Dynasty (206 B.C.-A.D. 24)), Yi Yin, China's earliest strategist and chief official of Tang, first king of the Shang Dynasty (c. 16th-11th century B.C.), twice advised his sovereign to come to grips with King Jie of the Xia Dynasty (c. 21st-c. 15th century B.C.) without resorting to arms before dispatching troops against him. The classic states that when King Tang of Shang wanted to undertake a punitive expedition against King Jie of Xia, Yi Yin offered his advice: "You'd better first stop paying tribute to him to see how he will react." King Tang stopped paying tribute to King Jie, who flew into a fury and moved troops of nine tribes subject to him to attack Tang. So Yi Yin told his sovereign, "The time is not yet ripe for us to undertake a punitive expedition against Jie. That he can still direct so many tribes proves that justice has yet to go to our side in its fullness." The next year King Tang, according to Yi Yin's advice, stopped paying tribute to King Jie of Xia once more. Jie was even more infuriated and once again asked the tribes subordinate to him to attack King Tang of Shang. But this time no one answered his call. And Yi Yin said, "Jie is completely isolated; now we can send our troops against him." King Tang of Shang sent his troops and soon overthrew the Xia regime, exiling Jie to one of the small tribes.

In business, this kind of reconnaissance may be desirable in the days after some trial-selling of a new product, if you want to know how the market will respond to its mass production. A case in point: The "White Rose" Brand washing machine trial-produced by the Yunnan washing machine factory was well received by the public, but whether its mass production would be worthwhile and what would be the right amount of it was still unknown. In order to solve the "riddle," the factory first came into grips with its 40 and more counterparts in Beijing, Shanghai, Guangzhou and other places by putting a batch of its products into the market and then decided on its production and operation policies, the scale of production and pricing on the basis of the outcome of the contest. From the very start, the factory placed high value on the quality of service, introducing the slogan "Customers First" into the factory regulations and taking for its knack of doing business guarantee to keep its sold products in good repair for a certain period of time, service given to the doorstep of the customer and "unquestionable warm-heartedness in dealing with even the least fault." Despite the fact that the "White Rose" was not of top quality and was inferior to many other washing machines in terms of the number of fuctions, it enjoyed many a favourable condition for development, as washing machines' service life was being prolonged in the country as a whole, the locally-oriented factory was backed by the Kunming electrical machinery plant well-known for the high quality of its products, and the factory was famous for good service and credit. Such being the case, the Yunnan washing machine factory decided that, so long as it will continue to improve the quality of its products and services, the "White Rose" will remain promising and can be put into mass production. From 1980 through 1982, the factory turned out over 11 thousand 3 hundred washing machines, realizing an output value of over 3 million yuan and a profit of over 300 thousand yuan. Life has shown the correctness of its decision and the success of its operation.

(C) **Using Espionage—Special Method of Collecting Intelligence and Information.**

Using espionage means sending spies to obtain the enemy's secrets—a means of military struggle. As the ancient saying goes, "In warfare, it is highly valued to know yourself and to know the enemy, and the enemy can be known only when espionage is used." To know the adversary by using spies is now a common practice in economic competitions, which is rife in the capitalist world.

According to the "Book of Espionage" compiled by Zhu Fengjia who lived in the Qing Dynasty (1644-1911), the use of spies goes back to King Shao Kang of the Xia Dynasty (c. 21st-16th century B.C.). The king sent his son Nü-ai as a spy to the State of Guo where Jiao ruled, and another of his sons Jichu to trap and kill Jiao's brother Yi, and finally ruined both the State of Guo and the State of Yi. Instances of using spies by the emperors, kings, generals and ministers of the successive Chinese dynasties were beyond counting.

According to "Biography of Lord Xingling" of the "Records of the Historian" written by Sima Chian (145 B.C.-? B.C.), one day Lord Xingling was playing draughts with the king of Wei (one of the seven states in China of the Warring States Period (475-221 B.C.)) when word was brought that beacon fires had been lit on the northern border and the King of Zhao was about to invade their territory. The King rose from the table to summon a council of ministers at once, but Lord Xingling stopped him and assured him, "The King of Zhao is only out hunting. This is no invasion." Presently another messenger arrived to confirm Lord Xingling's words. The astonished King asked Lord Xingling, "How did you know this, sir?" "Among my protégés are men who know all the secrets of the king of Zhao. They tell me at once what he is doing. That is how I knew."

To know the enemy in a military action, the use of espionage is of even greater importance than "observing the enemy" and "manoeuvring the enemy," for the information gained by observing or manoeuvring the enemy tends to be fragmentary and superficial, while the employment of secret agents entrenched in the camp of the enemy often yields "top secret" and "critical intelligence" obtained as a result of an extensive, careful observation over a long period of time. In "Sun Zi", Chapter 13, "Espionage," it is stated, "That the enlightened sovereign and the wise general always move and conquer the enemy and achieve feats out of the oridinary is because of their foreknowledge. This foreknowledge cannot be elicited from spirits and gods, nor can it be inferred from the analogy with anything experienced in the past, nor can it be tested and verified by the measurements of the movements of the celestial bodies. It can be obtained only from men who know the enemy situation." Here, the way to victory in a war cannot be clearer: Victory depends on foreknowledge of the enemy situation. Men who know the enemy situation are what we call "spies" or "secret agents" today.

The use of espionage is commonplace in the international

economic exchanges and the fierce competitions among companies and corporations of the present-day capitalist world. To overwhelm their competitors, the companies and corporations, on the one hand, found new research centres with all their technological power and huge amounts of funds, renew their technical equipment at the highest possible speed and turn out one new product after another to strengthen their competitiveness on the world market and, on the other, even more frantically, sparing no efforts and expenses, organize enormous networks of industrial and commercial intelligence agencies on a global scale in order to steal and ferret out the secrets of their adversaries, spot the weaknesses of their opponents and make the best of their own advantages to defeat the competitors. In an article on business espionage, the U.S. magazine "Time" quoted a noted expert in problems of security, as saying that in today's United States, small companies steal from big ones, and big companies steal from small ones, and people all steal from each other. According to the estimates of this expert, U.S. industrial and commercial enterprises lose as much as 20 billion dollars a year to theft of fruits of scientific research.

In the present-day world, the intricate business intelligence networks may very well rival the state and military ones in abundance of ways of using espionage, oddness of means of spying, broadness of the scope of activity and the preciseness of the intelligence obtained and the speed at which it is secured. There are cases when enterprises and corporations outstrip the government agencies and the press in quickness and accuracy in procuring new information. It is noteworthy, however, that the spying tricks resorted to by today's capitalist to cope with the ruthless competition remain those summarized by Chinese strategist Sun Wu over 2,000 years ago. "Sun Zi", ch. 13, "Espionage," points out: "There are five kinds of spies to be used. They are local, inside, coverted, expendable, and surviving ones." The only difference between today's spies employed by the capitalists and those of Sun Wu's days is that the former ones have modern science and technology at their disposal, and the means they use are by far trickier and more sinister than those of their ancient Chinese counterparts. Now let us take a look at some "new" ways modern capitalists use espionage in the light of Sun Wu's statement about five kinds of spies, so as to sharpen our vigilance and prevent ourselves from being fooled and cheated in dealing with them.

(1) Local spies. "Sun Zi", ch. 13, "Espionage", says: "Local spies are the enemy's country people we make use of." Where you are waging a war, there you get your agents from among the local residents. To know the movements of the enemy in proximity, direct observation, "giving him a stir," "making displays to entice him," or "probing him with a skirmish" will do. But to get information of far-reaching and wide-ranging significance from a considerable distance to serve your overall interests, you have to do something more than that. So, employing local spies, "the enemy's country people" who are in the know, will be the way to go. This is a common practice in the capitalist business, for it is often done in a legal form. For instance, to know all the goings-on in a given locality, a business engages there organizations or individuals concerned (workers of an enterprise, salesmen, local residents, reporters, diplomats, middlemen, business agents or brokers) to undertake for it observation for a special purpose and provide it with timely information. A certain electronics company in Hong Kong has its development department in Japan which employs a dozen Japanese technicians whose duty is to get hold of and pass on in time the information about the new techniques and new products of Japanese electronics industry and their samples. And the Company, based on the information thus obtained, develops new products of its own. In the United States, the Company undertakes joint development with American enterprises, the former bearing the costs of development and the latter being responsible for technological investment and formulation of product patterns. And the Company organizes production in Hong Kong accordingly. Both sides undertake to sell the products on the world market, while the American enterprises concerned draw their commission by the number of the pieces of products sold. It is believed that the speed with which certain Hong Kong electronics enterprises imitate the products of others and make their innovations is presumably linked with the presence of their overseas development intelligence agencies.

(2) Inside spies. "Sun Zi," ch. 13, "Espionage," states: "Inside spies are the enemy officials we make use of." What enemy

officials can be or may be bought over to become our spies? In his commentary on the ancient treatise in "Sun Zi with Anotations by Eleven Scholars," Du Mu pointed out that the following seven kinds of officials can or may: 1. Those who are able but have been removed from office; 2. those who have committed errors and have been punished; 3. those who enjoy favour and trust yet are greedy for wealth; 4. those who feel wronged as lower officeholders; 5. those who are denied credit with their superiors; 6. those who want to repair their impaired reputation by giving full scope to their abilities; and, 7. those who are shifty and deceitful double-dealers. Since China began carrying out her policy of opening to the outside world, some foreign businessmen have succeeded in employing in Guangzhou and some other Chinese cities a few of our government and business workers who had gone corrupt as their "inside spies." These people leaked out information on China's economy and technological achievements, selling it cheap, through correspondence, "contributions to the papers" "investigations abroad," "business discussions" with foreign merchants and in some other ways. We cannot afford to remain ignorant of and to relax our vigilance against such despicable tricks of the lawbreaking foreign businessmen.

(3) Coverted spies. "Sun Zi," ch. 13, "Espionage", states: "Coverted spies are enemy spies we make use of." There are two ways of using coverted spies: 1. to buy over the enemy's spies to our service, and 2. to make use of an enemy agent by pretending to be unaware of him and letting him get away with the false information we give him. Capitalist competitors widely employ this usual military trick of using the enemy agents. The United States, for one, resorted to this trick of clever use of an adversary's agent, pretending to be unaware and "leaving him at large the better to apprehend him," to defeat the attempt of the Japanese corporations of Hitachi and Motsubishi to steal the latest in the technology of the International Business Machine Corporation (IBM). The chief engineer of the planning section of Hitachi's Kanagawa plant lavishly bribed an IBM employee, from whom the Federal Bureau of Investigation (FBI) learned about Hitachi's intention of stealing IBM's secrets. The FBI, however, chose to refrain from getting IBM to bring a suit against the Japanese and, instead, sent an FBI old hand disguised

as an IBM expert and a company manager to deal with the Japanese engineer. The experienced and astute American spy finally defeated Hitachi in the "computer war" by luring his adversary with deceptive moves and baits. The U.S. trick of making use of a Japanese spy was referred to by the Japanese managers as "reconnaissance by laying traps."

Sometimes coverted spies are used in a covert way in a plot behind closed doors or in the clever diplomatic intercourses with smiles. Unlike average American managers who often decline visits or take a perfunctory attitude toward visitors, many Japanese company managers receive foreign businessmen and salesmen of other companies warmly and exchange greetings with them. The "hospitality" of these Japanese managers is meant, as it turns out, to help coax intelligence out of the visitors. The tactics is to avoid being sounded out by those who come to sound them out while sounding the visitors out and leaving them ignorant of that. This is also a kind of using "coverted spies," attack in the form of defence, picking up useful things on the sly without any trouble.

(4) Expendable spies. There are cases when the side using spies send them to provide the enemy with false information, and they are put to death when the deception is laid bare. These are expendable or doomed spies, who spread falsehood on purpose and thus lure the enemy into a trap and pay for it with their own lives. "Sun Zi", ch. 13, "Espionage", states: "Expendable spies are those of our own spies who are allowed to know fabricated information we have deliberatedly let out and report it to the enemy." The expendable spies are of two kinds. One, unconscious ones who believe the fabricated information given them by the decision-makers to be true and tell the enemy all that in a normal way and are put to death by the enemy who found himself taken in. In the years of the contention between Chu and Han, Liu Bang, King of Han, sent his advisor Li Shiji to persuade King of Chi to join Han. Convinced by Li, King of Chi relaxed his defense, and Han Xin, general of King of Han, broke into Chi with a surprise attack. Thinking that he was betrayed by Li Shiji, the raged King of Chi killed Li by boiling him in a big tripod. It was the role of an unconscious expendable spy that Li Shiji played. Two, conscious ones who thought nothing of their death

after a careful consideration, martyrs to a faith or those who repay their benefactors with their lives. There is no lack of examples of using expendable spies in military or political struggles, for strategic or operational purposes. In World War II, before the Japanese raid on Pearl Harbour, the Japanese government sent Kulusu, a man married to an American woman, to assist Nomura, the Japanese ambassador in Washington in the negotiations allegedly to define the respective interests of Japan and the United States in the Pacific Basin. This was a camouflage under which the Japanese slackened the Americans' guard and got information about them. Another example of the expendable spies is the "guide" sent by the guerrillas to get the enemy into a trap.

With the world-wide competitions turning white-hot, an enterprise may well be pushed out of the ranks of the competitors, which may cause its close-down or even ruin of families, if it makes a bad move in decision-making or falls behind even for a short while in technological development. Therefore, the enterprises and companies which are in the position of using extraordinary means for survival and development are not content with finding local spies, buying over inside spies and making clever use of coverted agents; they spare no pains and no expenses to train, send and use expendable spies. Instances of using such agents and their capture and punishment in business intelligence war are uncountable, if we extend the concept "spy" to mean all intelligence workers hunting for secrets of the adversaries by all illegal means. Take some statistics related to the Soviet Union, the U.S. and France. As has been reported by the press abroad, in the first half of 1982 alone, 23 Soviet secret agents were expelled by 13 countires, and within several days in late October that year the Western countries revealed two major cases of Soviet spies active in industry. In the United States, besides mutual stealing going on among the U.S. and other countries, the American enterprises steal from each other. According to a survey of 1,558 American companies, 1,224 of them confess that they use constant espionage against their opponents. Over one third of them have intelligence networks of their own. In one year the adversaries of the Gulf Oil Company stole from it several thousand kinds of materials about the new technology of oil extracting and refining, one of them being worth 1-5 million dollars. In France, large numbers of industrial spies have been caught each year since 1976. In 1980, there were 58,562 theft cases of industrial spies revealed by the French police alone, the losses caused by these thefts amounting to several billion francs. In France, a fashion association loses about 45 million U.S. dollars to the theft of production secrets. Although the expendable spies employed by various countries and enterprises have been "falling into the net," the latter never bother to slow the training of these spies or to narrow the range of their use because of this. Instead, their tricks of spying are becoming increasingly intricate and original. The reason is simple: The life of a spy is no more precious than that of an insect, considering the basic interests of the countries or enterprises concerned.

(5) Surviving spies. These are agents who can go to find out the enemy's situation and come back to report on it. "Sun Zi", ch. 13, "Espionage," states: "Surviving spies are those who return with information."

The use of surviving spies is one of the easiest ways of securing information. An enterprise may send its men for visits or tours, for furthering their study or doing practice, dispatch its experts to academic seminars or technological exchange meetings or do something like this—with the purpose of collecting information. The people sent may be carefully selected intelligence experts who know what's what in their "prey" at a glance and learn by heart what they chance to read, or ordinary staff members who are commissioned to visit a given enterprise or a given market in a given place with the purpose of collecting information by making inquiries and looking at this and that and, back at home, pool the data they have gathered for the information-processing workers to study and select from. The surviving spies, as a rule, employ overt means, and their actions are "open and aboveboard." According to Turkish newspapers, two "hazelnut spies" of West Germany have been reporting the quotations for Turkish hazelnuts to the West German hazelnut import and export corporations over the years, so that West Germany has been able to purchase the Turkish hazelnuts at relatively low prices. Every year when the hazelnuts ripened, the two German specialists toured Turkey's Black Sea coasts, places abounding in hazelnuts, to find out what was the prospect for that year's harvest and then they formed an estimate of the hazelnuts' export price and informed the German corporations concerned. For twenty-five years the two German have been at this job, bringing considerable profits to their corporations. They were the "surviving spies" in the service of the West German hazelnut corporations, agents returning alive with information.

The methods of using spies listed by "Sun Zi" have all been employed and are being employed by the capitalist business. Workers of socialist business management, we should learn to use local and surviving spies "on just grounds," " to our advantage" and "with restraint," attach importance to the use of coverted spies and see through the inside and expendable spies in the service of our adversaries. Only in this way can we deal with the lawbreaking foreign businessmen properly and defeat their plots.

The following five points deserve our serious attention in problems concerning espionage:

1. Choose the right intelligence agents. People competent both ideologically and professionally at the job of collecting information should be chosen and commissioned. "He who is able to make the wisest people his agents will make outstanding exploits."

2. Attach importance to coverted spies, but don't rely on them alone. "Sun Zi," ch. 13, "Espionage", says: "The sovereign must have full knowledge of how to use the five kinds of spies. Information must come mainly from the coverted spies, and therefore they must be given the most liberal treatment." In order to get hold of weighty intelligence materials to cope with the complex economic struggle and the international trade in particular, our business managers had better act in line with this teaching of "Sun Zi" about the coverted spies.

3. Strengthen our guard against spies. The knack of espionage lies in the ability to know your adversary without his knowing you. Our agents should always act in a legal way, with their intentions kept in top secret; otherwise, "what fails to be done brings harm." As regards the means and methods of espionage the adversaries may resort to, we must maintain sharp vigilance against them. To prevent leakage of secrets and loss of secret

materials, precautions must be taken against spies by way of seeing them through. As has been reported, leakage of secrets of China's patented traditional technology have reached alarming dimensions. Some of our enterprises know nothing of the importance of detecting and guarding against spies, which has caused the leakage of quite a few of our patented technologies and resulted in heavy losses. To cope with the industrial spies, to protect their interests and patent rights, governments of many countries of the world have established various anti-spy institutions, and the big corporations of the West themselves have been organizing and expanding their own secret services and procuring at huge costs the expensive electronic anti-burglary equipment. Therefore, the hundreds of thousands of Chinese enterprises and companies should also pay serious attention to the problem of taking precautions against and combating secret agents.

4. Using espionage, one should have a proper sense of cost. Money should not be begrudged where espionage of strategic significance is involved. Chen Ping, an adviser of Liu Bang, the founder of the Han Dynasty (206 B.C.-A.D. 220), did no small service to the Emperor's cause of contending with Chu by offering him wonderful strategic devises six times and thus was made prime minister and a marquis. One of his devises was: "spend a few tens of thousands of pieces of gold to sow dissension in the Chu army." Approving his plan, Liu Bang gave him forty thousand pieces of gold "to use at his discretion, not asking for any account." This shows that Liu Bang knew very well the need to spare no money for espionage purposes. This, of course, on no account means that our business managers of today may approve any item of expenditure at their own will. This only means that they should not hesitate to spend the money that has to be spent and give a free hand to the intelligence workers such as salesmen, information collectors and its analysts where it is necessary. Moreover, pros and cons should be weighed carefully, and the use of agents which may involve spendings exceeding the expected gains from the information it would bring should be abandoned. Thus, in case it is very difficult to obtain a certain patented technology from abroad, and at an exorbitant price at that, and a certain amount of investment in some research institutions and factories would be expected to yield a break-

through in working out that technology at home, use of spies should be given up, and self-reliance should come to the fore.

5. Sense of time is essential in information-hunting. A piece of late-coming information might bungle the chance of winning a battle and thus lead to defeat in a war. This is also true of the international economic contentions. A piece of timely information could sometimes help revive a business going to bankruptcy and, conversely, the missing of a piece of valuable information could be the beginning of the tragedy of a business. Time is the only touchstone for the value of information. Being one minute too early, the information would be dearer than gold; being one minute too late, it would be worthless like dirt.

3. Win Victory by Modifying Your Tactics in Accordance with the Changes in the Enemy Conditions

In Part 1 of this Chapter, we have pointed out the two principles for working out a plan: to know yourself and know the enemy; to win victory by modifying your tactics in accordance with the changes in the enemy conditions. In the previous two parts, we have focused on the principle and the methods of "knowing both yourself and the enemy", and now, let us go over to the problem of winning victory by modifying your tactics in accordance with the changes in the enemy conditions. "Sun Zi", ch. 6, "The Void and the Solid," states: "And as water shapes its course in accordance with the ground, so an army forges its victory in accordance with the enemy conditions. Therefore, there are no constant patterns of war, just as water has no constant shape. He who can win victory by modifying his tactics in accordance with the changes in the enemy conditions is considered divine."

In business management this means that one should formulate one's plan for operation in accordance with the changes in the environment, especially those in the market and the competitors. This has become a vital problem for business management, for in the conditions of the treacherous market and the life-and-death competition, the ability or inability of a business to adapt itself to changes would mean its survival or doom. The business managers should be good at working out plans for meeting contingencies in accordance with the changes in the market and the opponents in competition.

(A) Discard Fixed Rules and Change with the Changes in the Enemy Situation.

"To discard fixed rules and accommodate yourself to the enemy conditions", as is taught by "Sun Zi", means that every-thing, from the decision of the direction of attack and opera-tional policies to the execution of operational plans, should change with the changes in the enemy situation. In "Sun Zi with Annotations of Eleven Scholars," commentator Mei Yao-cheng said, "Actions should be taken according to rules but changed with the changes in the enemy situation, so as to benefit a decisive battle."

This principle is also one for a business to follow in its struggle for survival and development in an ever-changing environment. The manager of a multiple-operating company sponsored by the mining materials factory of the Benxi Mining Bureau who ran his enterprise as leader of some young people was good at following the market and the needs of the society and doing business and seeking development in line with the changing needs of the public. When people were keen on making sofas, and springs were in short supply, the company set up a spring factory with an investment of 1,200 yuan, and the customers were legion, bringing it a profit of 67,000 yuan in the first year of its work. When supply of springs exceeded demand, the manager, having learned that the people found it hard to get their clothes tailored and what sorts of clothing sold well, set up a clothing factory. This proved to be another success: the factory's products sold briskly in 15 provinces, yielding a profit of 34,000 yuan in just one year. Learning that some institutions in Benxi were in want of fuel-saving stoves because of a short supply of coal, the manager helped the young people to set up a factory of stoves for three purposes: heating, water-boiling and food-steaming. When he found that stores and stalls were too few in the city, he organized three shops and sixteen stalls run by the youth. By now his work has taken the company to staff of 1,300 employees, an annual output value of 2.6 million yuan and a total profit of 240 thousand yuan. This strategy of finding ways out by keeping abreast of the social needs and the changing market is exactly the strategy of "discarding fixed rules" and changing with the changes in the "enemy situation."

Now, let us take a look at a big enterprise to see if the same strategy works there as much as in the small ones. Let us look at the business strategy of the Hitachi Corporation, Ltd. of Japan, one of the biggest three Japanese corporations producing electrical appliances and an enterprise with a capital of 130 billion yen and a working staff of 70 thousand people. In Japan, Hitachi is well-known for knowing ways of operation. A middle-ranking official of Hitachi said in the connection, "As the main products of Hitachi are machines related to electric power, communications and transport, its customers are big enterprises. So, negotiations with the technical personnel of these enterprises are essential for our production, and we can never decide on what to produce and what to sell by ourselves. A producer who produces and sells what he himself prefers will be left with no profit." Namihe Odayira, the first chief manager of the Hitachi Corporation, laid down the guiding principle for production and operation of his enterprise: "The factory should turn out its products with the interests of the customers in mind, and the marketing units should promote sales of the products with the interests of the factory in mind." At Hitachi, "the production of even those goods the factory administration takes no interest in is to be continued and promoted, so long as there is demand for them." Small wonder that it is believed that the basic task for management is the management of change. It can be said that the principle of "discarding fixed rules and accommodating yourself to the enemy conditions" can help much in the "management of change" by business managers who react to change with change.

Then what are the points for attention in applying this principle to business planning? Firstly study the potential needs of the customer while keep the real needs of today's market in view; secondly, while designing a product and fixing plans for sales, take into consideration not only the substantials of the product such as its physical and chemical properties, but also the potential influence of the product or service on the customer felt in the brand of the product, reputation of the enterprise, preference of customers of various localities for one or another product, and the like; thirdly, remember that the needs of the market should not only be the basis for the product designing, regular production planning and sales planning in terms of quality and quantity, but also be the starting point and the end-result of the considerations about the structure of the enterprise, its financial budgets, personnel policy, the formulation of its rules, regulations and system of rewards and penalties, and many other things. In determining the strategic objectives, operational plans and organizational structure of an enterprise in the light of the principle of "winning victory by modifying your tactics in accordance with the changes in the enemy conditions," one may keep to the following working procedure:

1. Determine the operational objectives of the enterprise and the pattern of its products in accordance with the needs of the market, involving the questions of the varieties, amounts and quality indexes of the products to be turned out;

2. Determine the organizational structure of the enterprise on the basis of the operational objectives and the pattern of products decided upon, involving the questions of the acquisition of facilities, the organizational set-up, technical preparations, supply of raw materials, and the like;

3. Determine the size of the enterprise's personnel and the norms of appointments;

4. Determine the financial budgets, plans for revenue and expenditure and plans for gains and losses on the basis of the operational objectives and the organizational structure;

5. Form rules and regulations and a system of rewards and penalties, proceeding from the needs of production and the structure.

A vortical flow chart may illustrate the procedure mentioned above:

Chart 1
Vortical Flow Chart of Accommodating to the Changing Market

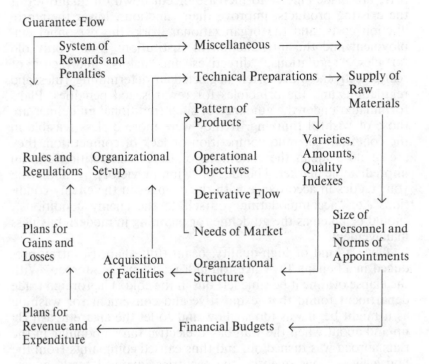

Two different flows are present in this chart: 1. the clockwise centrifugal flow starting from the needs of the market, or the derivative flow, as we call it, in which the general trend is that the preceding, or the inner determines the following, or the outer —a derivative, directive and restrictive trend; 2. the anticlockwise centripetal flow, or the guarantee flow in the authors' terminology, in which the general trend is that the outer depends on the latter and the following adapts itself to the preceding—a trend for subordinating, guaranteeing and promoting.

The principle of "accommodating yourself to the enemy conditions" as applied to planning and organization is diametrically opposed to the traditional guidelines of management and administration which focuses on "production" and directs chiefly production and under which changes in the operation of the enterprise are made chiefly to increase or cut down on quantities of the existing products, improve their functions, lower their production costs, and the organizational work, the personnel employment and the introduction of institutions follow only old "articles," "regulations," "directives" and "habits," and factors of real effectiveness are often neglected in determining rules and regulations and the principles for rewards and penalties. Plans formulated under the guidance of such traditional guidelines are those of wishful thinking. If they were more or less feasible in the conditions of mild competition or lack of competition, they are of no avail in the conditions of fierce competition and an unpredictable market. The idea of "winning victory by modifying your tactics in accordance with the changes in the enemy conditions", or "accommodating yourself to the enemy conditions", should be taken as the guideline for planning in modern business management.

Once a kind of high-quality, beautifully-shaped ashtray produced in Zhejiang Province found a ready market abroad. With the elapse of time it became left out in the cold. The foreign trade department found that, exquisitive and convenient for washing as it might be, it was too shallow and so let the cigarette ash fly up and about when the wall-based electric fan so popular in the flats abroad was turned on, and thus caused complaints from the housewives. Consequently, the factories involved made a new kind of ashtray with a small opening, a sizable belly and a deep bottom. The customers and the traders took great interest in it at once. Surprisingly, this new product became dull of sale several years later. The foreign trade department discovered through a new round of investigation that the wall-based electric fans abroad had given way to air conditioners in many homes abroad, and so housewives preferred the old ashtrays to the new ones which were inconvenient for washing. The Chinese factories made some improvement on their ashtrays and thus regained their market abroad. The story of the "rise and fall" of Zhejiang ashtrays shows that only reacting to change with change, "accommodating yourself to the enemy conditions" can a factory or a shop expect to see its products stay popular with the customers both in variety and in quality.

(B) Avoid Strength and Strike Weakness; Keep Your Initiative.

The essence of the principle of "winning victory by modifying your tactics in accordance with the changes in enemy conditions" as applied to business management is to emphasize the need for fixing quotas of production in accordance with demand. As the market represents the most multifarious demands, and the competitors on any one market, weak and strong, are of every description, no single enterprise can meet all the needs of the market, no matter what its size and strength are. So it follows that a business has to resort to a kind of selective tactics, if it is to meet the ever-changing demands of the market with its limited resources, to cope with various competitors and to develop itself the best. To avoid strength and strike weakness—this is the key to correct selection of the products or services to develop and effective competition with the opponents, a principle for winning the initiative in a passive position and mastering one's own destiny.

"Sun Zi," ch. 6, "The Void and the Solid," states: "An army's moves tend to avoid the solid and strike the void." By this statement Sun Zi meant that one should stay clear of the enemy's main force and strike at his weak points. In business decision-making, one would ask: what strengths to avoid and what weaknesses to strike?

(1) Stay Clear of Saturation.

When a certain product that an enterprise has made a monopoly of on the market for some time became unsalable, the wise decision-maker of the enterprise should stop or reduce its production. When the supply of a certain product that no enterprise has made a monopoly of exceeds demand, the business decision-maker should also reduce or stop its production on his own initiative. Take Huguang instrument plant in Shanghai for example. The plant had an annual rate of increase of its total output value at over 10 percent from 1979 through 1982, realized an output value of over 5 million yuan in the first half of 1983, an increase of 18 percent over that in the same period of the previous year, and turned over to the state over 2 million yuan in taxes and profit, an increase of over 50 percent compared with the same period of the year before. All this was due in part to the frequent adjustment of the products to avoid the saturation on the market. This the plant has been doing since 1980. It reduced step by step the production of the high-pressure electric bridges QS3, the capacitor bridges QS16 and the high-pressure capacitor bridges QS19 which had found a relatively saturated market and had become dull of sale, and rearranged their production in accordance with the demand stipulated in the contracts. Meanwhile, tapping its production potentials, the plant managed to turn out more of such products as the universal electric bridge SQ184, the DC steady-pressure mains yi44 and yi44A which were urgently needed by the state and sold briskly on the market.

(2) Stay Clear of the Strong Points of the Adversary.

Confronted with an outnumbering and overpowering adversary, the business manager should know that his only correct policy is to "fight when you can win, move away when you can't." In "Sun Bin's Art of War,"* another ancient Chinese military treatise, this "move-away" tactics is referred to as "*making way for might,*" one of the important 36 ruses of the ancient strategists, about which there is an old saying: "To move away is the best strategem." A business ought not to stake its future on any single product and manufacture it for ten or even twenty years on end. When one of its products becomes no more competitive, the business should "move away" to switch to the items needed by the market and yet unknown to other enterprises or far more competitive than the same ones of theirs.

At such a jucture, the wise manager should not stay content with what has been achieved; he should have an eye on some products he may develop next and have others on his mind.

The advantage of developing more kinds of products is that you can always find a way out of adversity by doing so. Thus, the factory of socks for children in Linfen City, Shanxi Province, extricated itself from predicament by following this line of operation. In the past, the factory had concentrated on one product only, which led to the overstocking of 110 thousand pairs

---

*Considered lost for centuries, this ancient treatise was discovered as recently as 1972 together with the bamboo slips bearing the text of "Sun Wu's Art of War" in a tomb of the early Western Han Dynasty on Yinqueshan Mountain in Linxi, Shandong Province.—*Trans.*

of socks by July 1981. Picking up tips from others, the factory soon gave up the old product as well as the old practice, and its work became active and fruitful as its production and marketing were well coordinated.

(3) Fill the Blank in the Market.

When you have the capability of meeting the special needs of the market or the customer for one thing or another, you should "fill the blank," "strike at the weak point" of the market. While the high-grade machine tools produced by the United States, Japan and Czechoslovakia found no market in Portugal, a country relatively backward technologically among Western nations, China successfully made her way into the Portuguese market with her own machine tools, middle-grade products by the international standards, as they were well suited to the needs of the Portuguese machine tool market in their properties, operation rules, pricing and quality. This is why the business agents are optimistic about the prospect of Chinese machine tools on the Portuguese market. Few countries are willing to make the small-calibre bearings much sought for, because their production involves large numbers of work hours, yet its profit rate is low. Taking advantage of its abundance of labour power and its fine processing technology, China's Loyang bearing plant chose to "fill the blank" by taking up the production of that sort of bearings, and the weight of this move has been felt on the world market.

(4) Strike at the Weak Points of the Opponent.

In competing with opponents of the same trade, you can strike at their weak points where you have enough strength to spare. Thus, in tendering for construction projects in the developing countries of the Middle East, the China Aviation Technology Import and Export Corporation came off victorious "in the very first game," entering the international construction market with success. Where did the key to their triumph lie? As Sun Wu said, "He who advances and cannot be resisted charges the enemy's void." The corporation, adhering to its guiding principle of "good faith, high quality, low profit and emphasis on ties of friendship," succeeded in getting the tenders it put in accepted one after another, with the business growing bigger and bigger. The decisive factors here were low-priced labour of the Chinese enterprises, low costs of construction, socialist planning and friendly quoted price. In 1983, the acceptance of the tender for one Syrian project alone brought the Corporation U.S. $776 million, a sum exceeding the total amount stipulated in the contracts for labour service export China signed in 1982.

(5) Show "the Void" or Weakness Where There Is "the Solid" or Strength, and Vice Versa.

There are cases when the market looks saturated, when overall predominance goes to your opponents and yet you possess some partial strength. Then you have to show your weakness where you are strong, or show your strength where you are weak in order to make a partial breakthrough and exploit the victory to change the overall situation. Thus, the Tonghai hardware and electrical appliances factory found that the dull sale of its high-quality electric irons which had ranked fourth in the nationwide appraisal of the quality of the same products was due to the fact that the factory was a small one and was paid little attention to by the nation's customers. The managers wondered how to open up a new prospect for their product. A careful study led them to the conclusion that, with the production costs of their irons being rather low, they could, "showing weakness where there is strength," adopt a policy of "small profits but quick turn-over" and "contract in order to expand" and in this way gain greater market for their product. So they had the gross profit from one electric iron reduced to one *jiao* (1/10 yuan), and thus they achieved what they wished: first their electric irons became famous in the province, then they found their own place on the national market, getting into Beijing and other big cities.

There are many ways to "show strength where there is weakness," the commonest one of them being the stratagem—"Attack in order to defend." Thus, some hotels with unoccupied rooms and enough bar and teahouse seats to spare claim in their notices and advertisements that those who are going to put up at these hotels or drink tea at the teahouses, or enjoy themselves at the bars, should first check in or line up for tickets, and then wait till notice. This is meant to make use of the people's psychology that "the harder to obtain a thing, the more anxious one becomes to obtain it." These hotels solicit customers by "showing strength where they are weak" and putting up a show of attack in order to defend, with the purpose of turning their weakness into strength and gaining more profit. Commercial advertisements often give examples of such a stratagem in the form of posters such as "Great Reductions in Prices." "The Last Batch on Sale. Don't Hesitate to Buy."

The principle of "avoiding strength and striking weakness" is only one of Sun Wu's basic ideas of winning victory by modifying one's tactics in accordance with the changes in the enemy conditions. As to the other important strategic ideas contained in "Sun Zi" which are applicable for the same purpose to business planning and the implementation of plans, such as the use of the irregular to win, the vital role of speed in war, the thesis that there can never be too much deception in war we will deal with them in Chapter Three.

4. Move when It Is to Your Advantage; Act when Success Is Certain

Every road leads to Beijing, but which is the best route for one who wants to go there from Kunming? Directly by air, or by train, or first by bus to provinces Guizhou and Sichuan and then by ship downstream along the Yangtse River to Wuhan and by train from there to Beijing? It would be hard to give an answer to this question, because the notion "the best" or "optimum" needs a qualitative restriction. If time-saving is taken as the prerequisite, the optimum would be non-stop flight by plane. If one wants to be somewhat thrifty with the travelling expenses, one would take the through train. If feasting one's eyes and enjoying oneself among beautiful mountains and rivers is what the traveller wants, he would choose a mixed type of travelling by means of transport of his own choice instead of travelling by plane or by train alone. Likewise, a manager makes his choice of business strategy in line with some criteria set for assessment and judgement. What are, then, the criterion in business management for judging of its strategic superiority and the success of its plans? Profit, or in the terminology of "Sun Zi," "advantage." Profit, meaning the long-range interests as reflected in the business strategy of an enterprise and the economic results to be expected when its plans are carried out.

Sun Wu stressed the need for advantages, which was of two kinds: the advantages in a battle and the gains in logistic support. He taught, "Anciently those who were renowned to be good at employing troops moved when it was advantageous to do so; and halted when it was not." (ch. 11, "The Nine Varieties of Battleground") "With no advantages available, do not move. With no gains in prospect, do not use your troops." The idea expressed in the two statements is one: engage the enemy when the battle is advantageous to you, and avoid engagement when it is not. Sun Zi also taught: "What is valued in war is the final victory, not prolonged operations." (ch. 2, "Waging War") He pointed out that "the cost of such materials as ... will reach twenty thousand or more taels of silver a day. A one-hundred-strong army cannot be raised unless such a sum of money is in hand." Here, gains, or material interests of a state, are at stake. In business management, they mean economic results, a problem of the relationship between input and output, between what is expended and what is gained. Sun Zi's ideas of advantages, or interests, or gains, as the primary concern for waging a war should also guide our business management in which "interests," "profit," "gains," "economic results" should be given prominence to as the chief factor in making decisions.

Moving when it is advantageous to do so and acting when success is certain, you are advised to pay attention to the following six kinds of relationships:

(1) The Relationship Between the Microcosmic Benefits of an Enterprise and the Macrocosmic Benefits of the State.

An enterprise should see its fundamental interests and the basis of its survival and development in the maximum satisfaction of the needs of the society. The interests of the enterprise and its workers and staff hinge on the overall interests of the state, and their welfare depends on that of the state. In socialist China, the capitalist greed for gains at the expense of reason and principle should be rejected. When the interests of an enterprise are found in contradiction with those of the state, the former should be subordinated to the latter. In handling the problem of distribution of benefits among the state, the enterprise and its workers and staff, the interests of the state should come first, those of the enterprise the second, and those of the individual workers and staff members the last.

(2) The Relationship Between the Immediate Interests and the Long-term Ones.

Profit is one of the indicators of the economic results of an enterprise and should be gained with the utmost efforts. However, problems like the reform of the enterprise and the training of qualified workers may crop up and conflict with the gaining of the immediate benefits of the enterprise. In that case, the manager should use his reason to make a careful analysis of the situation and handle the contradiction properly, taking account of both the immediate and the long-term interests. As a business leader, he should take a long view of things, fix his attention on the future, and avoid trying to save a little only to lose a lot. What he needs is foresight and sagacity.

(3) The Relationship Between the Interests of the Consumer and Those of the Enterprise.

Since the product is intended for the consumer, to meet the needs of the market and to gain profit for the enterprise are the two sides of one and the same coin. An enterprise gets some profit by meeting the needs of the consumer with its high-quality and low-priced products in latest styles and in great variety. A manager should always remember that only what contributes to consumption contributes to the survival and development of the enterprise. Otherwise, when, for instance, you sell low-quality products, or you sell your goods at exorbitant prices, or your service is bad and repulsive, the customer will decline to buy, or refuse your service. And then, your plan for gaining profit will come to naught. The only way to go is to "help others and help yourself," to benefit the society and receive the support of the society for the growth of your business.

(4) The Relationship Between You and Your Opponents in the Question of Gains.

Competition between enterprises is in essence an activity to seek "profits." But, seeking profits, one has to have a sense of propriety, depending on who one is dealing with. The principle for gaining profits is applied somewhat differently to international trade and domestic trade. In China's domestic trade, quite a

few enterprises keep to a socialist way of doing business beneficial to others and to itself and the state alike, directing its
technological advantages to the development of new products
and thus avoiding scramble for gains with similar enterprises,
though they possess considerable supremacy for competition. In
socialist China, competition between enterprises cannot exclude
cooperation and mutual benefit. Take the question of pricing. In
case the state gives the right of pricing to individual enterprise,
and the managers of an enterprise cannot be sure of the size of
the expected profits from a product or a service, they may get
just the opposite of what they wish—either fail to get what they
wish or lose what they has gained. If they set a price too high for
a certain monopolized product, other manufacturers and trading
companies will become envious and try their best to take your
monopoly away. If the price is set too low, it will cause difficulty
for the its upturn in the future, for the customer will cut down
on the consumption of the product in favour of its substitutes
because of the price rise and thus leave the enterprise without
even the minimum reasonable profit.

(5) The Relationship Between Quality and Production Costs.

Considering the long-term and overall interests, one of the
prerequisites for the survival and development of the enterprise
is incessant improvement of the quality of products or services.
But while deciding on the specific qualities of a product and
arranging the production, one must not forget that good quality
should go hand in hand with economy, with the expected gains.
To think that the higher the quality, the better, is as one-sided
and harmful a view as to think that poor quality of a product is
just a trifle. While it is unadvisable to pay little attention to the
quality of a product which would lead to steady reduction of
sales, it is also wrong to overstress quality which would result in
the rise of production costs and the weakening of the competitive
power of the enterprise.

(6) The Relationship Between Gaining Profit for the Process
of Production and Operation as a Whole and Gaining Profit for
Individual Links and Stages of That Process.

The process of production and operation of an enterprise is
one of unification of production, supply and marketing, one of
coordinated use of human, financial and material resources.

While the enterprise should "move when it is advantageous to do so," each stage and each link of the whole process of production and operation should also do so, keeping in view the interests of raising the economic results of the enterprise as a whole. This is why campaigns for increasing production and practising economy are launched, technical innovations are made on a large scale, rational production processes are organized and the democratic management by the workers and the staff is practised. And the harmony of the interests of various stages and links is also essential. Only with that can partial advantages be turned into overall advantages, or overall interests, or expanded economic results.

5. Concentrate Your Forces Against the Enemy and Seize the Right Moment to Act

A good decision may prove worthless because of improper use of resources and ineffective implementation. A manager's responsibility for decision-making does not end with the determination of the orientation and the objectives of business and the operational plans by means of preliminary estimates, acquisition of knowledge of both his enterprise and its adversaries, modification of his tactics in accordance with the adversary's situation and taking account of the expected gains. His responsibility should also include decisions on moves directed to the implementation of his plans, i.e., programmes for action. Such a programme should encompass the following points: the procedure of the realization of the operational plans, arrangements for the use of resources, discipline and regulations binding upon all members of the enterprise in the implementation of the plans, specific targets fixed for all the subordinate units, technical and organizational measures to be taken, and so on and so forth. The programme for action is meant to make clear about the direction of the use of the enterprise's resources, their amounts and qualities required and ways of using them, and to define what is to be done, how, and by whom. There are a lot of ways of using an enterprise's resources correctly and effectively—human, financial, material, technological resources and intelligence and information to be directed to a desired goal in right amounts and in right proportions. Here we would like to discuss only one of these ways: "concentration of your forces against the enemy," as it is taught by "Sun Zi." Chapter 11 of the treatise, "The Nine Varieties of Battleground" states: "What is essential in directing a war is first to pretend to act as the enemy's designs require and then concentrate your forces to strike at the enemy at one point, killing his general even with a long drive of one thousand li. This is known as achieving one's goal by ingenuity."

And how the idea of "concentrating one's forces to strike at the enemy at one point" is to be understood as regards business management and applied to it correctly?

(A) Seize the Thing to Do and Concentrate Your Forces on It.

In " 'Sun Zi' with Annotations of Eleven Scholars", Du Mu said, "Once you have spotted where the enemy's weakness manifests itself, you should resolutely direct your concentrated forces to hit at it. Thus, you can capture the enemy's general even with a long drive of a thousand li." in business management, "to concentrate forces to strike at the enemy at one point" means, to put it simply, to go all out to do what is certain to succeed, or "to set to something decided on with the momentum of an avalanche. Early in 1980, having learned that our shoe factories were in want of China-made highly-efficient milling machines for making shoe-trees, the Kunming Machine Tools Plant decided to start their production at once. With the gauging of a chosen imported machine being done by some best designers of the plant, they formed an assembly line for such machines before long and started their trial production. Only eight months were spent on turning out 60 milling machines for making shoe-trees, all of which were soon sold out at a sales exhibition sponsored by the Ministry of Light Industry at that plant. After that, the plant organized the production of 130 main machines and sold 129 of them and 230 auxiliary machines at the national sales exhibition of machine tools and instruments held in Wuhan in October 1982, with a profit of over 2 million yuan which comprised nearly 50 percent of the plant's 1982 gross profit. What is noteworthy is that, based on the market information, the plant decided that the national market for shoe-trees-making mill machines will become saturated by the third quarter of 1982 and stopped their production while the Wuhan exhibition was still going on. Sure enough, no more orders for such milling machines were placed with any one of the three plants exhibiting them in Wuhan during the days of the exhibition, despite their heavy advertisement on TV, on radio and in the press. The managers of the Kunming Machine Tools Plant were praiseworthy indeed for their skills of making decisions. How they excelled at getting hold of market information, putting all their efforts into what they were certain of, concentrating their forces on it and seize the right moment for action. In business management, however, the principle of "concentrating forces" is not to be applied mechanically, in a stereotyped way. It is good for some activities of an enterprise, such as the solution of technical difficulty, the work on some invention or innovation and the grasp of a key technology, but it is no good for others such as the organization of the day-to-day production, because "concentration of forces for a battle of annihilation" would lead to disorder in production, low quality and high costs.

(B) Select the Right "Breakthrough Point" and Concentrate Your Forces on the Main Direction of Attack.

In his work "Problems of Strategy in China's Revolutionary War," Mao Zedong pointed out: "In my opinion, when we face a powerful enemy, we should employ our army, whatever its size, in only one main direction at a time, not two. I am not objecting to operations in two or more directions, but at any given time, there ought to be only one main direction." ("Selected Works of Mao Tze-tung", Eng. ed. FLP, 1964, Vol. 1, p. 236) In order to get the best economic results by satisfying the needs of the market with the limited resources of an enterprise, its managers cannot but concentrate their forces on the main direction of attack at the right moment. First, they should be clear about the two different notions: the operational objectives of a business and its main direction of attack. The former is the objectives a business intends to achieve in a given time: what products it has to offer the market? What it wants to get from the market and in what an amount? The latter involves the question of where the enterprise is to direct its main forces to ensure the fulfilment of its plans after the objectives are fixed. Owing to the fact that enterprises differ in their position and internal conditions, that factors affecting or determining the fate of an operational plan also differ with different enterprises, their "main directions of attack" will never be completely the same, and they may be even totally different from each other. With the Yunnan "Baiyao"* factory, for instance, since the supply of its Camellia Brand Yunnan "Baiyao" awarded with a gold medal by the state lagged behind demand on domestic market and enjoyed good reputation abroad, the managers put stress on the further improvement on the quality of the product to keep its fame untarnished and the increase of production with reduced costs to attain better economic results instead of sales promotion. As for the Yunnan Chemical Engineering Machinery Plant situated also in Kunming, since its main products had been the necessary accessories for minor chemical fertilizer machinery which found little market in 1979 when the country adjusted her national economy, the managers put advertisement, promotion of sales of the plant's serialized products, and manufacture of the pressure vessels on the top of their agenda, besides intense study of the province's new needs for chemical engineering machinery and ways of developing new products. So it can be seen that each of the two enterprises mentioned above had its own "breakthrough point" and went its own way to success, concentrating its main forces on the "main direction of attack" it chose for itself.

(C) Lure the Enemy to a Desired Position.

According to Jia Lin, one of the commentators of "Sun Zi", the military principle of concentrating one's forces against the enemy can have another meaning. Jia Lin wrote: "One can capture or kill the enemy's general even at a distance of one thousand li by luring the enemy forces with gains to where one wants them to go." In modern warfare, this is called: "to lead the enemy by the nose," or "to serve as the enemy's chief of staff." That is to say, one must manoeuvre the enemy instead of being manoeuvred by him. In business management, this method of luring the "enemy" to a desired position is also applicable. While

---

*A white medicinal powder for treating haemorrhage, wounds, bruises, etc.—*Trans.*

an enterprise must fix its production quotas according to the prospect of sales, organizing production in accordance with the needs of the market, the society and the state, it can, in certain circumstances, "lead" the market "by the nose" and arouse the interest of the market to buy its products. As is witnessed by the history of human civilization, new inventions have always brought forth and satisfied new needs of the people. This indicates that production and scientific experiments should not be aimed at merely satisfying the people's basic needs, that new products should be developed to make the market prosper and advance in the direction desired. "Leading the market by the nose" can be of great use to the operation of an enterprise; it can be done and it should be done. Statistics shows that many successful pharmaceutical factories turn out new medicaments comprising 50-70 percent of their total output each year. The new products arouse the people's interest to try them, and thus sales of the factories' products are promoted and their revenues increased. This is to create new products, create new market, create new demand, starting from scratch. It should be noted that enterprises successful in doing so have all concentrated their human, material, financial and technological resources and their facilities on the new products after a careful investigation of the market and a feasibility study of the technological and economic aspects of the projects. Making contribution to the development of the society and the enhancement of human welfare, such enterprises make great headway themselves. So not without reason is it said that only the enterprises capable of creating the new can survive in the fast-changing world. Anything useful for men and beneficial to the society "led the market by the nose," i.e., created a market, when it first appeared in the society or first stimulated the people's demand on entering the market. Examples of such new things are myriad, ranging from steel needles and screwdrivers to trains, steamships and space shuttles.

So far we have dealt with the five basic phases of business decision-making and planning in the light of the military treatise "Sun Zi": Reckon and scheme before a battle with the knowledge of both the enemy and yourself; Find out the enemy's situation first in order to win victory ; Modify your tactics in accordance with the changes in the enemy conditions; Move when it is to your advantage and act when success is certain; Concentrate your forces against the enemy and act at the right moment. Ending Chapter 1, we would like to stress that since business operation is a process of development in ever-changing conditions and so plans often prove to be in disparity with the realities, and the longer the interval between plan-making and the realities you face, the bigger the gap between the two, making estimates and decisions cannot but be a never-ending process of adjusting and balancing various relations to tally your tentative plans with the objective realities as best as possible. And this process covers decision-making, organization of production as well as competition for market. Does the business activities of an enterprise end with the realization of the objectives of its operation? Yes, and No. For with the end of one phase of business activities begins another, and it will always be so.

Chapter II
To Make Yourself Invincible Before Fighting a Battle and Organize a Proper Administration of Your Collective
—Things at the Core of Production Management

Reckoning, or making estimates, comes first in waging a war. But, in business, objectives, policies and plans, attractive as they may be, would remain on paper without a well-managed, competitive organization capable of giving good-quality products. Hence the need for the study of production management.

"Sun Zi," ch. 4, "Positions", states: "In ancient times those skilled in war first put themselves into the position of the invincible and awaited the moment of the enemy's coming into the position of the vincible" and "a victorious army seals its victories before seeking battle, whereas an army bound for destruction fights in search of a victory." That means that one should be well prepared before engaging the enemy in a battle instead of fighting on the off-chance. Another ancient military treatise "Sun Bin's Art of War" also stressed the need for "acting only after the completion of preparations." It held that "only with real preparedness can an army make military exploits in its expeditions and return intact," otherwise, "anyone fighting without proper preparations suffers losses." This has always been a vital law of military operation, according to which "there is no need to talk about war, if an army has no certainty about its victory; and there is no need to talk about attack, if an attack is not certain to bring about the downfall of an enemy stronghold."

As regards business management, the process of making an enterprise itself invincible spans the conceiving of a product, its designing, manufacturing, discharge from the factory and meeting with the customer or competitor. This process is divided into two stages: the stage of planning and the stage of the implementation of the plans. The latter in turn consists of two links: production and marketing of the products, both guided by the operational plans already fixed. Of the two links the one connecting business plans with marketing is production, key to shaping the strength of an enterprise to ensure its invincibility before a "battle." So it follows that only with a proper management of production can an enterprise be managed effectively.

To do a good job of production management means to do a good job of the organizational work and coordination inside the enterprise on the principle of "acting only after the completion of preparations," with the sole goal of turning out competitive products needed by the market, and thus to bring about a situation ensuring success for the enterprise. "Sun Zi" discussed time and again the organizational work related to human, financial, material and other resources. In the light of the theses of the ancient treatise, we are going to deal with three problems in the organization of the productive activities of an enterprise: "the creation of the optimum situation and the build-up of energy and momentum," "the proper management of a collective" and "the choice and employment of chief commanders."

1. The Creation of the Optimum Situation and the Build-up of Energy and Momentum

"Sun Zi," ch. 5, "Momentum," states: "A master of war seeks his victory from utilizing the situation...." And again: "A skilful commander develops a potential like that of round boulders rolling down from a mountain height." Obviously, by the Chinese word "shi" (   ), Sun Zi meant chiefly two things: situation, or compelling circumstances available taken as a whole; and "potential energy, or power, or irresistible momentum." Round boulders rolling down from a mountain height with the momentum of an avalanche are irresistible indeed.

To create a situation and to build up huge momentum of action which will make your victory a certainty is also a question of primary concern for business management. To do that means to enhance the quality of an enterprise, to get the various aspects of its work into the optimum situation through effective productive, operational and managerial activities, putting the "round boulders" of the products and the services of the enterprise, as it were, on the "mountain heights" of the market to wait for the right moment to "roll down" and overwhelm every competitor in their way.

Therefore, the concept of creating the most desirable situation and building up energy and momentum as applied to business management comprises two things: the goal and the means of doing so. The goal of doing so is to help realize the targets of the operation of the enterprise by getting its production, services, sales promotion and competitive power into the optimum situation. The means of doing so is the enterprise's effective productive and operational activities as well as organizational work, all aimed at bringing about the optimum situation.

So far as production management is concerned, two things are to be paid serious attention to in the creation of the optimum situation: to act in accordance with the law of productive activities and the law of economic activities and to bring about rational organization of production in terms of the use of resources.

(A) Act in Accordance with Objective Laws.

"Sun Zi," ch. 6, "The Void and the Solid," states: "Military tactics is like the flow of water, for just as flowing water avoids where it is higher and rushes to where it is lower, so an army's moves tend to avoid the solid and strike the void. And as water shapes its course in accordance with ground, so an army forges its victory in accordance with the enemy conditions." Here Sun Zi expounded the law of war in a simple language with the help of the law of flowing water, which is an eloquent, universally true argument applicable also to business management.

The study of business management involves productive force, production relations and superstructure. In terms of "objective laws" (like that of the flowing water), there is much to be studied in the socialized big production with strict division of labour and meticulous cooperation, in the integration of human, material and financial resources, time and information, in the coordination of various links of production, supply and marketing, in the organization of production in accordance with the set technology of production. Modern big production would be impossible and people would have to swallow the bitter fruit of their own misconduct, if there were no centralized management, no attention paid to the objective laws of managment and no organization of production in accordance with the requirements of the production process for continuity, right proportions and rhythmicity. In the area of circulation, objective laws are also to be studied, such as the law of commodity production, the law of value, and the like. In the production relations and the superstructure, certain laws should also be observed, laws involving questions such as those of the "five key factors"—"the Right Way, heavenly timeliness, ground, command and institutions," discussed by Sun Zi.

Business management in our enterprises has witnessed no lack of instances of suffering from violation of laws of productive and economic activities: casualties caused by neglect of safety in production, overstocking of low-quality products and the resultant waste caused by pursuit of quantity at the cost of quality in production, financial disasters in capital construction as a result of violation of the essential procedure of work in favour of simultaneous surveying, designing and construction, output of shoddy products from neglect of balanced production in favour of doing a crash job by throwing ·in all the physical labour, facilities and materials available at the end of a month, a season, or a year, and even fabrication of false reports on the output of products in case of failure to fulfil production quotas.

(B) Effect Rational Organization of Production as Means of Creating the Optimum Situation.

Where does the optimum situation of an enterprise in terms of production, marketing and competition come from? It comes from rational organization and correct command, from management by building up energy and momentum.

"Sun Zi," ch. 5, "Momentum," states: "A master of war seeks his victory from utilizing the situation and does not make excessive demands on his men." A skilled commander creates the optimum situation and wrests victory of war by relying on his own talent for organization and command and favourable circumstances, instead of demanding victory of his subordinates. This is what is referred to as managment, or government, by building up energy and momentum.

The same chapter also states: "Generally, management of many is similar to management of few. Structure and organization are the key to it." And again: "Order or disorder is determined by organization." In organization and command Sun Wu saw a means of creating optimum situation and management at the service of a skilful military commander.

Sun Zi stressed the role of actual strength in creating the optimum situation. "Sun Zi," ch. 3, "The Strategy of Attack," states: "To conquer the enemy without fighting is the height of excellence." To achieve this, one must invariably rely on his favourable situation and his actual strength, no matter the enemy is under siege or not. One must create a situation favourable to himself and unfavourable to the enemy with the strength at his disposal and every means available. "Sun Zi," ch. 4, "Position," states: "A conquering army is like scores of catties weighed against a tael; an army destined to defeat like a tael weighed against scores of catties." The conquering army wins by throwing into the battle its overwhelmingly superior power, by utilizing its favourable situation and actual strength. The actual strength of an army hinges on the quality of its officers and men, and its weaponry and equipment.

An enterprise wins a competition also by its actual strength. It has also to consider how to "weigh its scores of catties against a tael" and how to create a situation favourable to it. The strength of an enterprise depends chiefly on its quality conditioned by three factors: management, technology and personnel of which the leading body is the most important part. Judging by the capacity an enterprise manifests, the quality of an enterprise means its capacity for the development of new products, for extended reproduction, for opening up new market, for training and enlisting people of ability and for conforming to changes. To raise the quality of an enterprise, therefore, means to raise its managerial level, its technological proficiency, the quality of its personnel and, above all, that of its leading body. All these efforts are devoted to the creation of an optimum situation facilitating the realization of the enterprise's operational objectives by means of much-needed products of fine quality and moderate prices, best service and highest commercial credit.

"Sun Zi," ch. 5, "Momentum", contains many statements about how to organize effective military activities, such as "Generally, management of many is similar to management of few. Structure and organization are the key to it. And commanding many is similar to commanding few. Banners and signals are used for it." "When a large army succeeds in withstanding the enemy's attack without suffering defeat, it is the tactical use of the irregular and the regular that makes it possible." "When troops overwhelm the enemy with the momentum of dashing a grindstone against an egg, it is caused by the right use of the solid to attack the void." These statements of Sun Wu call respectively for paying attention to organization and command, doing a good job of communication and liaison, manoeuvring troops for both "regular" and "irregular" attacks, and avoiding strength and striking weakness in a battle. All these teachings are of basic importance for business management which, like a military operation, owes much to correct organization for its success.

The military treatise "Sun Zi" also gives quite a number of expositions on the organization of military supplies: "An army which, lacking impedimenta, provision and supplies, will be lost." (Chapter 7, "Contention for Advantages") "Generally, military operations require one thousand light chariots, one thousand heavy ones, one hundred thousand mailed soldiers and provisions transported for a thousand li. Then the expenditures involved both at home and at the front, including those for the entertainment of state guests and envoys, the cost of such materials as glue and lacquer and the money going to the maintenance and repair of chariots and armours, will reach twenty thousand or more taels of silver a day. A one-hundred-thousand-strong army cannot be raised unless such a sum of money is in hand." Here Sun Wu spoke on two essential points: the importance of logistics which is vital to war, and the need for rational organization of the complicated work of military supplies. "Those well versed in the art of war do not raise a second levy of conscripts nor require to be again provisioned." "It is due to distant transportation that a country is impoverished by military actions." "A wise general will see to it that his troops forage on the enemy." "What is

valued in war is the final victory, not prolonged operations."
(Chapter 2, "Waging War") These statements of Sun Wu's do not
deal with logistics as such, nor do they discuss the organization
of military supplies in general. They stress ways to raise the
"economic results" of the war, ways to support the war with a
minimum of human, material and financial resources and win
quick and great victory. Apparently, Sun Wu's ideas of creating
optimum situation and commanding by building up energy and
momentum would give us much food for thought and some
examples of action to model after when it comes to the study of
business management, rational organization of production and
operation, and enhancement of the quality of the enterprise and
its economic results.

2. The Proper Management of a Collective

The proper management of a collective of men is to a business
what management of state affairs is to a state, management of
military affairs is to an army, and management of a household
is to a family. It is a thing of vital importance.

The creation of the optimum situation which we have just
discussed in the preceding section of this chapter, means the
creation of superiority in production and operation through the
organization of men, facilities, materials and other contributing
factors. And it is men who are the creators and who hold sway
over all the productive and operational activities. As has been
mentioned before, an enterprise is an economic organization
offering the society the products and services it needs and setting
as its object the maximum output by a minimum input of
resources, manpower, raw materials and equipment. And it is
men who hold the key to the conversion of what is put in into
what is put out to meet the needs of both the society and the
enterprise. The fuller play given to the intellect and talent of men
and their initiative, the greater the probability of the output
exceeding the input. So it follows that one of the main tasks for
business management is to effect a proper management of men,
or a collective of men. All successful managers have been found
skilled at managing men as a special kind of resources.

(A) "Unite the People with Their Sovereign in a Common Aspiration;" "He Will Win Whose Officers and Men Are United in Their Wishes."

Anything to be done has its purpose. At an enterprise, men are managed for the purpose of achieving increased output through mobilization of their enthusiasm. Whether men's enthusiasm can be mobilized and to what a degree depends largely on their own free will. Only when the managers' objectives are in keeping with the will of the managed can men's enthusiasm for work be given full play to. This is exactly what the ancients meant by saying: "It is acting in accord with the people's wishes that causes governments to prosper; it is acting contrary to people's minds that causes them to fail," (Guan Zi, ?-645 B.C.) and "Heavenly timeliness is not as important as the advantages of the ground; the advantages of the ground are not as important as harmony in human relations." (Mencius, c. 372-289 B.C.) Sun Wu expressed the same idea with the phrase "to follow the Right Way", or "to be on the side of a just cause." A just cause enjoys abundant support while an unjust cause finds little suport, as a Chinese saying goes. "Sun Zi," ch. 1, "Reckoning," states: "By 'the Right Way' is meant the cause which unites the people with their sovereign in a common aspiration so that they will live and die for him without fear of danger." To "unite the people with their sovereign in a common aspiration," the latter should follow a correct basic line and carry out correct guidelines and policies, so that one hundred generals are of one mind, and all the three armies coordinate their efforts, and the troops are anxious to fight and invincible. As for business management, to effect such a unity presupposes not only correct guidelines and objectives of operation but also the conscientious adaptation of the individual goals of the workers and staff to the general objectives of the enterprise. To achieve this, the following ideas and practices of management would be essential:

(1) Look After the Workers' Interests.

Marxists hold that what people strive for is all related to their own interests. The fundamental interests of our people lie in the emancipation of the working class and the prosperity of the nation. Apart from the fundamental interests, there are the interests of the collective and those of the individual to be looked after. Motivation of men is closely linked with their interests. When motivation becomes one with interests, there is motive force. Common interests of the leader and the led are the foundation of their harmony. As "Sun Zi," ch. 3, "The Strategy of Attack", pointed out, "There are five circumstances in which victory can be foreseen: ... He will win whose officers and men are united in their wishes". In socialist China, "to be united in wishes" means to be united in the common effort to bring prosperity and strength to the nation and well-being to the people in the drive for the realization of the modernization programme. Strengthening our politico-ideological work in this spirit, it is a must to gratify the individual needs of the labourers. To conduct production efficiently, an enterprise must mobilize the producers' enthusiasm for work through politico-ideological work as well as material incentives so that they concern themselves with the fruit of their labour, which has a direct bearing on their own material interests. This reflects the unity of means of management and objectives, "Gratify the needs of men, and they will work toward what is needed"—such is our conclusion.

To gratify the needs of men, one should first know what these needs are. In modern management studies, the need hierarchy concept developed by the American psychologist Abraham H. Maslow is quite popular. He divided men's needs, or desires, into five levels: 1. The physiological needs, which are the most prepotent, including those for material supplies indispensable for sustaining one's life, for the protection against starvation; 2. the security needs meaning a sense of a secured life and the prevention of body injuries and the like; 3. the social needs implying the need for love and affection, for friendly feelings from and toward others, for belongingness to a group; 4. the esteem needs embracing those for self-respect and those for being respected by others; 5. the need for self-actualization meaning the desire for achievement by way of maximum self-development, creativity and self-expression. From these views of the "behavious science" we, on our part, can draw on something useful for our business management after a critical study in the light of the Marxist tenets.

In the socialist enterprise, the socialist principle of material incentives must be adhered to.

As a rule, the satisfaction of the workers' reasonable demands for material benefits contributes to the growth of production, and the failure to link production with the workers' material needs would lead to the loss of their interest in production, which damages the enterprise itself. A business leader should carefully study the question of how to "gratify the desires" of individual workers and those of the enterprise's personnel as a collective. What all the workers and staff members demand in a given period of time constitutes the common disire of the collective. The enterprise that knows this common desire of the collective well and excels at directing it will "sail right before the wind". Conversely, an enterprise that ignores the common desire of the collective and lets things drift will "run aground" because of the reaction of that desire or its lack of regularity.

The "common desire" of the workers and the staff is of both material and spiritual nature and is conditioned by both the circumstances inside the enterprise and the social environment. It varies with the changes in time, place and circumstances. A manager should shoulder the responsibility of grasping these changes, adapting himself to them and solving the problems of meeting the growing material and cultural needs of the people better, in good time and on his own initiative. In the early post-Liberation years and the period of the First Five-Year Plan, the common desire of the workers was to build socialism as masters of the state in the conditions of having ample food and clothing. Since the late 1970s, the workers and staff members of the enterprises, yearning for the realization of the modernization programme, have shown more interest than before in the distribution of material benefits such as wages, bonuses and housing. The business managers who understood such common desires and managed to satisfy them properly in time, have always succeeded in boosting production in their respective enterprises. Those who failed to do so, either ignoring the reasonable material benefits of the workers and demanding work along of them in the "Leftist" way, or advocating the doctrine of "Money comes first in everything" in the spirit of Rightism, in total disregard of the Party's Four Cardinal Principles, have always undermined the workers' enthusiasm for production or caused demoralization or even conflict between the leader and the subordinate.

Apart from the "common desires" of the workers, the desires of individuals are also to be taken into account, which plays a special role in business management. Particular demands of individuals have much to do with the common desires of the collective, as the latter is based on the former, and differences in age, family background, character, experience and position among the people bring disparities in their individual demands. The satisfaction of the individual demands works much more quickly than that of the common desires of the collective. Thus, give a young couple of newlyweds a flat, or adopt an innovation an old engineer has developed with decades of painstaking labour, and they will be gladdened beyond description and will work even harder than before. Fail to do so, and they will feel depressed, weighed down with care, and will have no heart to do their work. So a manager should study the general trend of the workers' individual demands as well as their common desires, and take into special consideration the demands of the key members of the technical personnel and the people whose role is essential to the enterprise, and satisfy them by adopting necessary measures.

(2) Show Love for the Rank-and-File and Reward One as an Example for All.

Concern on the part of the manager for the managed is of vital importance. The military treatise "Sun Zi" contains quite a few discourses on this subject. For one thing, it lists "humanity" as one of the indispensable qualities of a general. What is the reason, then, for the fact that in some cases this concern for the managed brings little or no result and is even rejected by them? The answer lies in the attitude of the manager himself. Different attitudes lead to different actions—showing loving care or pity, giving a helping hand or alms, commending or flattering—and give different effects. Sun Wu believed that only with a feeling like that of father and son and that of brothers can the commander and his subordinates be united in mutual attachment and trust. In Chapter 10, "Terrain", of his treatise, Sun Wu said, "Regard your men as infants, and they will march with you into the deepest valleys. Look on your soldiers as your beloved sons, and they will risk death with you." This idea of commanding troops by love lay and lies in the foundation of the success of all the eminent generals, in the past and today. Wu Chi, a brilliant general of the State of Wei in the Spring and Autumn Period (770-476 B.C.), "ate and dressed like the rank and file. He slept without a mat, marched on foot instead of riding on horseback or in a chariot, carried his own rations and shared all his troops' hardships. When one of his men had a boil, Wu Chi sucked the pus from it." (See Sima Chian: "Records of the Historian") In the Red Army led by the Chinese Communist Party in the 1930s officers and the cooks alike carried baskets of grain on a shoulder-pole into the mountains and got the same share of "mess savings", money saved out of the daily mess expenses for pocket money. For the manager to share weal and woe voluntarily with the managed serves the purpose of promoting harmony between them, getting them together in a common cause through unanimity of actions and feelings and thus ensuring the attainment of the objectives of the collective. The idea of showing love for the rank-and-file and commanding troops by love can mean something new in the business management of socialist China where the fundamental interests of the manager and the managed are one and the same. A manager of our enterprise should concern himself with many things important to the workers and the staff members—their livelihood, their joys and sorrows, marriages and funerals, education and entertainment, their children's enrollment in schools or employment, etc., and try to lend a helping hand as best as they can. While it is an abnormal practice characteristic of a petty producer for a business manager to get his enterprise to take over all the functions of the whole society, it is a necessity dictated by the development of the enterprise and the needs of the society and at the same time the unshirkable duty of the manager to concern themselves with and show love for the workers and the staff, helping to solve various questions in their daily life and thus freeing them from cares.

Giving awards to model workers is a common practice to show love for people. Sun Wu said in Chapter 2 of his treatise: "It is the prospect of being rewarded with wealth that prompts them to take booty from the enemy." Soldiers who do so should be rewarded with material benefits. In business management, awards should be given to those who have done much for the growth of production, especially the advanced workers who have made outstanding contributions. "Reward the soldier who captures the first of the ten or more chariots taken in a chariot fighting," said Sun Wu in that same chapter. The manager must see to it that awards go to those who deserve them by hard work and penalties to those who deserve them by indolence. He must avoid partiality in giving awards, keep those of no merit from being rewarded and prevent a share-and-share-alike approach. Only in this way can he encourage those left with no awards by "rewarding one as an example for all" and get people to achieve what is desired by the enterprise.

(B) "Manage Them with Civil Virtues and Unite Them in Action with Martial Authority."

It is believed that management is a process in which one exerts his influence on others, that management is a force, a force of control, which one possesses and exercises onto others. A manager can find a lot of ways of exerting his influence and exercising his authority for control—guidance, supervision, material incentives, moral encouragement. To show love for the rank-and-file, to reward those of merit and to gratify the people's desires means to guide and encourage—a kind of force of initiation which leads people to progress. And supervision is a kind of driving force urging people to push forward. Both force of initiation and driving force serve to stimulate people, and the manager should be good at wielding both of them, guiding, urging, stimulating people to do their best. The manager should learn to get both of these forces into motion in one and the same direction and advance his business without a hitch by adjusting relations between men and coordination of the departments of the enterprise.

(1) Rule by Both "Civil Virtues" and Rigor of Discipline, with Due Reward and Punishment.

As an army without a strict discipline is useless in a war, so an enterprise without a scientific management and a set of regulations and disciplinary provisions favourable to the development of production can never operate as it should do. To satisfy the demands of the producers must not be understood as unprincipled accommodation or tolerance of abuses. To satisfy the people's desires and to get the people work toward what is desired represent a unity of the aim, motivation and means of management. If the managed are interested solely in personal gains and indifferent to the interests of the state and the collective, if they seek only benefits from the collective in disregard of discipline, the love and care shown for them by the manager would cease to play a positive role and would even bring harm. In other words, if the force of initiation applied by the manager under given conditions for a given period of time fails to work or gives little effect with part of the people, the manager should deal with them with some necessary means in order to avert danger to the common cause. "Sun Zi," ch. 10, "Terrain," states: "If you give your troops liberal treatment but cannot employ them; if you love them but cannot make them obey your commands; if there is disorder in your troops and you cannot bring them back to order, they may be likened to spoiled children, and are ineligible for use." In that case, the commander should see to it, among other things, that the troops be accessible to command and control. And one of the measures to be adopted toward that is the enforcement of some disciplinary provisions and regulations to curb transgressions, guide the conscientious people and give the unworthy people admonition. This is the way to push the collective of both the manager and the managed forward along the right path to their common goal.

The manager can use the force of initiation and the driving force simultaneously or alternatively, depending on the circumstances. They are what is referred to as "civil virtues" and "martial authority" in the military treatise "Sun Zi." In its Chapter 9, "Marches," it is stated: "If soldiers are punished before they turn loyal, they will not be obedient. Disobedient, they will be hard to employ. If soldiers, having turned loyal, refuse to subject themselves to punishments, they cannot be used. Thus, manage them with civil virtues and unite them in action with martial authority, and victory can be guaranteed." In his commentary to "Sun Zi", ancient strategist and sovereign Cao Cao (A.D. 155-220) wrote: "Civil virtues imply humanity, and martial authority—law and discipline." As regards management, to "manage with civil virtues" means to carry on political and ideological education among the managed so that they can be clear about what is right and what is wrong, what is just and what is unjust, and to "unite in action with martial authority" means to keep the people in step by enforcing law and discipline. Success will be ensured, if the two things are done. Then, when are "civil virtues" more preferable, and when is "martial authority"? To give an answer to this question, it would be to the point to cite the following story from Chinese history. In the period of the Three Kingdoms (A.D. 220-265), a lot of people in the Kingdom of Shu complained about the rigour of Prime Minister Zhuge Liang's political measures. A man named Fa Zheng told Zhuge: "Anciently, the First Emperor of the Han Dynasty proclaimed a three-point law on entering the seat of the overthrown Chin Dynasty, and the people there were very grateful to him. So I hope you, Mr. Prime Minister, will soften your penal code and relax your prohibitions and restrictions so as to appease the people." Zhuge Liang's reply was: "You don't know the difference between then and now. The Chin rulers indulged in abuses and harsh punishments, and the people resented them to a degree that they readily responded to the call of one man to rebel. In consequence of this, the three-point law of the Han Emperor could help much to put him on the throne. But, in our times, Liu Zhang, the former ruler of Shu, who was ignorant and incompetent, could neither effect the measures beneficial to the people, nor keep the authority of the penal code. As a result, the rich and powerful ran amuck, the sovereign and his officials ceased to be their own selves, and all desire for hard struggle had left them. In such circumstances, the remedy must be suited to the case, and now government of Shu needs the enforcement of rigorous laws and decrees. This will let the people know what good rigorous laws and decrees can bring them. And official ranks and titles should be offered with restraint, which will honour those who are offered them. Thus, the people will be benefited, the officials will be honoured, and there will be order and discipline in the relations between the ruler and the ruled. And this should be given top priority in the political programme of the state." Zhuge Liang's brilliant statement graphically demonstrated when "civil virtues" are preferable, and when "martial authority" is. People of later generations commented much on this score. A pair of famous couplets hung in the Memorial Temple of Zhuge Liang in the city of Chengdu, Sichuan Province, serves as the best commentary on the above-mentioned statement of Zhuge's. It reads: "Conquer the heart of the foe, and disloyalty will be no more; so since ancient times masters of the art of war have never been warlike; Seize the right hour for showing tolerance or severity, or else either will prove of no avail; so future rulers of Shu had better think it over." These couplets present a pertinent interpretation of Zhuge Liang's most important idea of management: There are two ways of management of men: that of "tolerance" and that of "severity", i.e., that of "civil virtues" and that of "martial authority"; and which one to follow depends on judging the hour and sizing up the situation correctly, otherwise neither will be a success. Therefore, the principle of judging the hour and sizing up the situation correctly is what rewards and punishments should be based on. Both Sun Wu's idea of "managing with civil virtues and uniting in action with martial authority" and Zhuge Liang's principle of proper handling with tolerance or severity according to the situation can be made use of in our business management.

To handle management and administration with proper "tolerance" or "severity", the following points might as well be taken into consideration:

1. Base your rewards and punishments on facts and impartiality, mete them out just as they are deserved. A personal enemy who merits a reward must not be ignored, and your own flesh and blood deserving punishment must not be spared.

2. Prevent rewards or punishments due from missing, no matter what minor reasons have caused them. At the same time, excessive rewards or punishments are to be avoided, for they indicate lack of rules of management and therefore absence of management itself.

3. Meting out rewards or punishment, special attention should be paid to the persons and incidents that are of considerable significance to the overall situation. Rewards due to the rank-and-file must not be left out, and punishments deserved by generals must not be rescinded. In the period of the Three Kingdoms, Zhuge Liang, Prime Minister of the Kingdom of Shu, sent his officer Ma Su to fight a battle at Jieting with Zhang He, general of the Kingdom of Wei. Ma Su led his troops away from the river to go uphill, making a fatal strategic mistake, and Zhang crushed Ma's army by cutting off its grain supply and

seized Jieting. Zhuge Liang refused to forgive Ma, his old friend who had made meritorious service before, and, with tears, had him imprisoned and executed. Cao Cao, famous military commander and statesman contemporary with Zhuge Liang, ordered in a march that whoever trampled down the people's crops should be executed. But he himself unwittingly broke his order as the horse he rode, startled by a flying bird, leapt into the field by the road. Cao Cao then "cut his hair in punishment of himself", which made a great impact on his troops. The two examples of punishment cited here caused then quite a stir and gave favourable effect because it was given to persons of importance to the situation.

A business manager who can reward and punish in this spirit can make his work a success. Director Wang Zepu of the seamless steel tubing mill of the Anshan Iron and Steel Complex said, "Comrade Deng Xiaoping put it well that criteria for rewards and punishments must be made perfectly clear. Otherwise, I believe, nothing can be done in an enterprise." Wang, taking charge of the security and health work of his mill, laid down regulations for public health with criteria for rewards and punishment stipulated in them. Once, an inspection group sent by the leadership of the Complex came to check up on the sanitary conditions of the mill and specially found fault with the spots neglected by a thorough cleanup. They found dust in the granary and asked the director of the mill if this was where health work had failed. "Yes. Then fine me first," replied the director. And the 20-yuan bonus for that month was taken away from him, and other nine leaders were also deprived of their bonuses. Then the workers did their best to improve on their sanitary conditions and brought their mill to the fore in this respect. By punishing himself and other leaders of the mill, Wang Zepu showed the need for strict observation of discipline for all. Under the impact of this move of the director, the mill made great headway and soon stood out from the iron and steel plants of the country.

(2) Put Your Troops into Desperate Straits.

"Sun Zi," ch. 11, "The Nine Varieties of Battleground," states: "To assemble the army and plunge it into desperate straits is the duty of the general." To throw the army into a peril in order that it will fight to the death with a doubled energy born of the great straits it finds itself in is a method of managing the troops and encouraging them to crush the enemy with all their might, as advocated in "Sun Zi." Business management knows similar ideas and practices. Apart from discipline and regulations as a means of pushing the managed in the direction desired, which is well-known and routine, there is another means of urging people to exert themselves in their work, which can serve as a strong stimulus and give immediate, strong effects. And that is the idea of putting the army into a desperate position, as was expounded by Sun Wu, known in the science of management as moral stimulation and "rescue" management. By moral stimulation is meant the practice of triggering men's motivation and producing strong impact on them by making use of the particular effect of a particular situation and particular conditions on people. By "rescue" management is meant the practice of tapping the potentials of the managed by making use of the disastrous conditions available. In the foundation of this method of management lie the following argument: Anyone, when faced with disaster, can handle things much faster than could be imagined, show an ability unknown before and raise his efficiency of work to the utmost. Moreover, "rescue" management implies managerial steps taken on the manager's own initiative on the basis of his foresight and intended to touch off what is imminent, rather than a mechanical reaction to an unexpected disaster. Disasters, understood in a broad sense, include all sudden incidents and expected events bringing danger to the cardinal or specific interests of the state, the enterprise and its personnel. It is the duty of the managers to discover a potential disaster as early as possible, bring it to light in good time for all to see and make timely decisions to cope with it. This is "rescue" management in action, with the potential energy of the managed mobilized and "twice the result with half the effort" achieved in management.

"Sun Zi," ch. 11, "The Nine Varieties of Battleground", also points out, "Put the troops into an impasse and they would rather die than flee in defeat." Put into a desperate position, the troops have no alternative but to fight for life at any costs. Therefore, the commander should, at the moment of necessity, go out of his way to throw his troops into adverse circumstances to give full play to their courage and martial ardour in the battle. As Sun Wu said in the same chapter of his work, "In a severe peril the soldiers fear nothing; finding no escape, they will be firm; ... when faced with no alternative, they will fight to the death ... when put into an impasse, they will display as much courage as that of Chuan Chy and Tsao Kuei*." Thus, we can see that the so-called moral stimulation and "rescue" management in modern science of management were expounded by the Chinese strategist Sun Wu more than 2,000 years ago. And they were successfully practised by noted generals of ancient China. According to "Records of the Historian," General Han Xin, attacking Zhao, sent ten thousand men to form ranks in front of the river. When the men of Zhao saw this, they laughed heartily thinking this was against traditional art of war. But once the troops drawn up before the river joined battle with the superior Zhao forces, they fought stubbornly and could not be defeated, and finally they won the battle. The officers asked Han Xin what strategy it was to form ranks before the river, Han said, "Does 'The Art of War' not say, 'Put them in a death trap and they will come out alive; send them to destruction and they will survive'?" Han Xin's strategy was exactly one of moral stimulation, when he pitched his troops in front of the river against the superior forces of the enemy so that, in a desperate position without any chance of retreat, his troops went all out to fight for their own survival and won despite the extreme danger they had been put in.

Enterprises abroad have increasingly adopted moral stimulation and "rescue" management as means of arousing the enthusiasm of the managed and promoting business. The Hitachi Corporation of Japan, for example, resorted to this strategem to cope with the recession overtaking it in the 1970s as a result of the oil crisis prevailing in the capitalist world. The company decided to send 675 thousand workers of 24, or two thirds, of its plants home for the latter half of 1974, with 97-98 percent of their pay issued as before. This created a sense of critical moment among the workers and the staff, though the economy it brought was insignificant. In January 1975, the corporation deepened the sense of crisis among its managerial officers by cutting back on

---

*The exploits of these heroes are recounted in the Chapter "The Assassins" of "Records of the Historian".—*Trans.*

the wages of 4,000 of them, the harshest measure ever taken since the corporation's founding. In April that year, the corporation put off the date of the newly recruited workers' taking up their jobs for 20 days, causing a sense of emergency from the very start of their work and a sense of critical moment among other workers and staff members. These steps taken by the company helped to urge people work even harder and to put its business back on its feet more quickly than was the case with other Japanese companies. The final accounts of the Hitachi Corporation made in March 1975 showed a drastic reduction of its profits to 8.9 billion yen, only one third of the 28.1 billion registered in the final accounts in September 1974, while the Toshiba Corporation found its profits decreased from 13 billion to 5.4 billion yen. Of the two corporations, Hitachi suffered a heavier loss. But by September 1975, Hitachi found its profits doubled to amount to 17.5 billion yen, whereas Toshiba had a 49 percent decrease of its profits, netting only 2.8 billion yen. The latter half of 1975 saw Hitachi's profits rising to 24.4 billion yen, 73 percent of those of the same period of 1973, the year before the recession. Toshiba had an upturn, too, but it recovered only 40 percent of the profits it had gained in the latter half of 1973.

In socialist China, the relationship between the manager of the enterprise and the managed is essentially different from that in the societies of private ownership. In our enterprises, the manager and the managed are all their masters, and their differentiation is but of a relative character, a necessary division of labour called for by the socialized big production. As all the workers and staff members, masters of the enterprise, work for the increase of economic results for the society as well as the enterprise and for the benefit of their own, they need not force themselves to work, much less cheat and bluff themselves. This constitutes the essence of the matter. Nevertheless, one can never overemphasise the importance of a correct understanding of the prevailing circumstances to the formulation of a correct policy for action. It is necessary for every worker to be clear about the situation the enterprise and he himself are in and his responsibility for helping develop what has been achieved and avoid stagnation and retrogression of the enterprise by his hard work. It is the duty of the manager to explain the situation of the enterprise to the workers, make the gains and losses known to them and reveal the essence of things for them. And the role of education is not to be underestimated in this connection. In our enterprises, the managers should conduct education among the workers to enable them to know both tomorrow and today, both the prospect of the huge progress of socialist construction and the backwardness of science and technology and underdevelopment of economy in China today, and they should make it clear that unless the present situation is changed, the nation will suffer at the hands of foreign powers and the people's material and cultural life will remain at a low level. All this can exert a mental pressure on the workers, urging them to work for the modernization drive with a greater zeal. Some appropriate measures can also be adopted to produce a "sense of emergency" in part of the enterprises or among part of the workers of an enterprise, such as the closedown, suspension, or merging of some enterprises which have suffered losses for a long period of time, or their switch to other lines of business, the halt of production for a shake-up in some workshops or teams or groups which have failed to boost their production and their efficiency, coupled with withdrawal of the bonuses, deduction of pay and change of managerial workers. In many parts of the country and in many of her enterprises, these measures have already been put into effect. Although it may give rise to some difficulties, it is good for the overall interests of the country and the people.

(C) Be Good at Enlisting Help in Management

Anyone has only limited ability. Studies show that people who can be commanded directly and effectively by one person number only around six. This is what is called by the management researchers as the principle of management span. What if one has to manage sixty, or six hundred, or six thousand, or sixty thousand people with his meagre personal ability and energy? Then the extension of his ability and energy is needed, and so the help of things like organization, communications and regulations is to be enlisted. No wonder it is said that the key to good management is to enlist help. Here, we would like to discuss how to apply the methods of "enlisting help" mentioned in the military treatise "Sun Zi" to business management of today.

(1) Enlist the Help of Organization.

A worker's performance is judged by the result of what he has done with his hands. If he is made leader of a group, It is judged also by the result of the work of his group. As a group leader, he manages mainly by his own performance: he commands with his work instead of his words, and he can deal with troubles and problems which have cropped up by setting to work himself. This method of management—getting to work personally, taking the lead in the work, or working for somebody else—can be useful in "the management of few", but not in "the management of many." Once the group leader is made chief of a workshop or director of the factory or manager, he will be helpless with his old method of management: he can never work for the hundreds of a workshop, still less the thousands of an enterprise, no matter what a great ability he may have. And this is where management skills come in. "Sun Zi," ch. 5, "Momentum," states: "Generally, management of many is similar to management of few. Structure and organization are the key to it." In other words, it is a matter of enlisting help, a matter of relying on the functioning of organizations at different levels. An army of ten thousand can be divided into three divisions of three thousand each and one detachment of one thousand directly under the army leadership; a division, in its turn, can be divided into three regiments of one thousand each; a regiment—into three battalions of three hundred each and one detachment of one hundred; a battalion —into three companies of one hundred each; a company—into three platoons; a platoon—into three squads and a squad—into three groups. In that case, in an army of ten thousand, the number of people under direct command of one person ranges just from 2 to 4. This is management through organization, management by leaders at one level higher keeping an eye on leaders at one level lower without the former having to attend to everything personally. Such a method of management can enable a military leader to have as many troops as possible under his command and keep them in good order, and, likewise, a business manager to know how things stand in his big enterprise with a complicated structure and handle things with ease.

Dealing with the organizational structure, one should see to it that the number of its administrative levels be reasonable and adequate. If they are less than needed, difficulties will arise in administration; if they are too many, there will be a considerable rise in the costs of management and a drop in management efficiency resulting from difficulties in keeping the various levels of the structure in touch with each other and keeping them under control. Principles to follow in fixing the organizational structure of an enterprise are as follows: 1. Proceed from reality, from the size of an enterprise. Have more administrative levels in a big enterprise, and have less in a small one. 2. Determine the "management span of a manager according to his ability. Make it larger for an abler manager and make it smaller for a less able one. 3. Decide on your structure in accordance with the means of management available. With advanced communication facilities, fix a larger management span for an individual; otherwise, fix a smaller one for him. Administrative structure common in China are of three kinds, the commonest of them being the three-level one consisting of the general headquarters, workshops, and teams or groups. Bigger enterprises and companies have a four-level structure: the company headquarters, the factory headquarters, workshops and teams or groups. Smaller factories have a two-level structure: the factory headquarters and teams or groups.

Troops are usually organized as various services and arms —there are artillery troops, the corps of engineers, etc. It is also the case with business management. There are three types of the administrative structure of an enterprise: 1. The function-oriented structure which is determined by the technological process of production in an enterprise in the form of, say, a foundry shop, a metal-processing shop, a cold working and riveting shop, a product-assembling shop, etc. in a mechanical works. 2. The product-oriented structure which consists of workshops of certain products and departments of services in an enterprise of multifaceted production such as a pharmaceutical factory made up of a workshop of glucose, a workshop of berberine, etc. 3. The administrative structure with division of units by region when a corporation has its enterprises or companies located in various regions, provinces or cities, and with these units divided in their turn into workshops and teams or groups according to their functions or types of products. An enterprise chooses for itself one or another of the three types of administrative structure, or the combination of the three, or that of the first two, which is even more preferred, after a careful study of the various factors within it and without.

While relying on the administrative units at all levels, a manager should attach importance to the role of some "unofficial organizations" which mean collectives of a few coworkers which have been formed by chance. They may be "unions" of old schoolmates, old colleagues, or fellow townsmen, or "unions" of several young people of the same interest. Management researchers have discovered that when people fail to satisfy their need for community organizationally, through measures adopted by their leaders, there will be an increase in such "unofficial organizations." Some managers follow a policy of "nonrecognition" toward them and reject them as a "liberal tendency" and a nonorganizational activity; others take a laissez-faire attitude toward them and let things slide. Neither of the two approaches is correct. Such "unofficial organizations" have always existed and will exist in the future. They may play a passive role, counteracting the normal steps taken by the leadership or spreading some rumours, or the like. Yet they may also be made to play a positive role in the growth of the enterprise when guided and directed properly. And this is important for a manager. It is said that the "unofficial organization" and the official organization of a collective constitute the two parts of a pair of scissors, and the bisector of the internal angle between the two indicates the direction of the movement of the collective. The easiest way to keep an "unofficial organization" under control is to find out and get hold of its influencial figures such as Liu Sijia in the Chinese TV play "All the Colours of the Rainbow."* It goes without saying that the "unofficial organizations" referred to here are natural, habitual communities in normal conditions rather than illegal factions and groups undertaking political activities.

(2) Enlist the Help of Means of Communication and Command.

While the contradiction between the limited capacity of the manager and the multitude of the managed is handled by organ-

---

*Based on a Chinese novel of the same name by Jiang Zilong, Panda Books, Beijing, 1983.—*Trans.*

ization, other contradictions have yet to be tackled. Because of the needs of production, marketing and services, many enterprises extend their activities to many regions, counties, provinces or even countries; with the scope of business enlarged, the distance of communication between the manager and the managed lengthens, and, with the competition becoming more and more acute, the time for making decisions shortens. Difficulties arising from all this are beyond the strength of oranization alone. "Sun Zi," ch. 5, "Momentum," gives a simple remedy: "Commanding many is similar to commanding few. Banners and signals are used for it." That is to say, numerous troops are directed into a battle with the help of "drums and bells" and "flags and banners." "Sun Zi," ch. 7, "Contention for Advantages," states: "Voices cannot be heard in battle, hence the gongs and drums; the troops can hardly see each other in battle, hence the flags and banners. Gongs and drums, flags and banners are used to command the hearing and sight of the troops." They are used to overcome the time and space barrier between the commander and the soldiers in battle. In business management today, the manager can likewise extend his ability with the help of the means of communication offered by modern science and technology such as communications satellites, electronic computers and various means of transport of our times. Modern science and technology can make the manager well-informed and well-versed in "remote control" as never before.

Management of people by enlisting the help of organization and means of communication and command has always proved its value for a country, an army and an enterprise alike—for any collective of people since ancient times. "Records of the Historian" tell the following story: Sun Wu gained an audience with King of Wu on the strength of his military theory. "I have read all thirteen chapters of your book," said the king. "Will you train a few troops as an experiment?" "Very well," replied Sun Wu. "Will you try with women?" "If you wish." The king sent him one hundred and eighty beauties from the palace, and Sun Wu divided them into two companies with the king's two favourite concubines as their leaders. Having made them take up halberds, he asked, "Do you know the front from back and your left hand from your right?" The women assured him that they did. "When

I give the order to advance, go forward. At the order 'Left!' turn towards your left hand, at 'Right!' turn towards your right, at 'Retreat!' turn back." The women assented. Having laid down these rules, he had executioners' swords and axes made ready and repeated his instructions a third and yet a fourth time. Then with the roll of a drum he gave the order "Turn right!" The women burst out laughing. Sun Wu said, "If the rules are not clear and orders are not understood, the commander is to blame." Once more he repeated his instructions a third and a fourth time, then beat drums and gave the order for a left turn. But once more the women burst out laughing. Then he said, "If the rules are not clear and orders are not understood, the commander is to blame. But when orders are clear yet not carried out, it is the officers who are to blame." He prepared to execute both company leaders. The king, watching from his stand, was aghast to see that his favourites were about to be executed and hastily sent messengers with orders, saying, "I can see you are able general. But without these two concubines my food would lose all flavour. I beg you to spare them." Sun Wu replied, "I have been appointed commander, and a general in the field is not bound by orders from his sovereign." So he had the two leaders killed as an example, and made the next two officers. This time, when he sounded the drums, the women turned left or right, advanced or retreated, and knelt or stood up exactly as they were told, not daring to utter a sound. Then Sun Wu sent a message to the king, saying, "The troops are in fighting trim, ready for inspection. Your Majesty can do what you please with them—they will go through fire and water." The story gives a vivid illustration of Sun Wu's three principles of managing people: 1. management by organization, as he divided the 180 women into two companies with the king's two favourite concubines as their leaders; 2. management by means of communication and command, as he beat the drum and gave his order; 3. management by rules and discipline, as he laid down his rules and repeated them many times and had the two leaders who had failed to carry out his orders executed. The result of Sun Wu's management was that the women acted exactly as they were told when the drums were sounded again.

Similar things occur in our daily life. For example, a factory in the suburbs of a city had the children of its workers transported by bus downtown to their schools everyday and put them under the care of a girl who was a worker of the factory. Enthusiastic about her job as she might be, she found herself helpless with part of the little ones always making a row and behaving badly, and soon she "resigned". A woman worker who had been a teacher replaced her and managed the children quite well despite her older age and poorer health. The secret lay in her knowledge of organization and the use of the means of command. She divided the children into groups with the elder ones as their leaders who acted as were told and directed them to go on or off the buses and to march or halt by blowing a whistle. So this was successful management.

(3) Enlist the Help of Laws and Regulations.

Besides organization and means of communication and command, laws and regulations and various institutions are also essential to management.

"Sun Zi", ch. 10, "Terrain," states: "... if there is disorder in your troops and you cannot bring them back to order, they may be likened to spoiled children, and are ineligible for use". That disorder cannot be brought under control arises from lack of laws and regulations or the lax enforcement of them. Therefore, rule by law is needed. We must have laws to abide by and have their violaters prosecuted.

"Sun Zi" contains a lot of statements on laws and regulations. The treatise opens with emphasizing "institutions" meaning "laws" or "methods" as one of the "five key factors," and raising the question "Which side is capable of enforcing regulations and orders more rigorously?" as one of the seven "comparisons." The "institutions" of Sun Wu's has a manifold connotation implying, among other things, laws and regulations.

It is in Chapter 9, "Marches," that "Sun Zi" makes the significance of laws, regulations and all necessary institutions clearer than in any other chapter. Apart from the statement "Manage them with civil virtues and unite them in action with martial authority", it says, "If your orders have always been consistently enforced, your instructions given to the troops will be obeyed by them. If your orders have not always been consistently enforced, your instructions given to the troops will not be obeyed. That orders are enforced consistently indicates the harmonious relationship between a commander and his troops." Here, Sun Wu stressed that orders can be obeyed only if the soldiers have always been taught to obey them, and only when they are obeyed can there be harmony between a commander and his troops—a forceful argument about the importance of observation of law and discipline.

When we discussed Sun Wu's idea of "managing with civil virtues and uniting in action with martial authority", we interpreted "civil virtues" from the viewpoint of "humanity" and "martial authority" from the viewpoint of "law." Actually "civil virtues" imply also rites and music, rules and regulations, and "law" implies also cardinal ethical code, and they supplement each other in management. All in all, laws and decrees, rules and regulations are all of vital importance to management.

We have discussed the role of organization and means of communication and command in management. And we must not forget that all of them depend on laws, decrees, rules and regulations for their functioning. Companies and groups of the ancient troops were units provided for by some organizational regulations, and their flags and banners, gongs and drums were just means of unifying command. Sun Wu wrote, "Order or disorder is determined by organization". And organization depends on military orders, discipline, regulations and all other institutions.

"Without rules one cannot draw even a square or a circle," says an ancient Chinese proverb. The story of Sun Wu training the king's maids points to the role of rules. With an enterprise, only regulations and discipline can keep its activities going on without a hitch, make the hundreds or thousands of its workers keep step with each other, introduce order into the daily chores of the managerial work, and ensure the seriousness, continuity and effectiveness of management. Enlisting the help of rules and regulations to make up for his limited ability and energy, a manager can rise above his daily routine and set his heart on his chief duty of planning and scheming, leaving the day-to-day work in the hands of his subordinates who handle everything according to regulations and precedents.

While establishing and perfecting an enterprise's rules and regulations, one must proceed from its realities, avoid excessive-ness and mechanical imitation and entrust the job to a single department of the enterprise such as the office of the headquarters or planning office, so that people know whom to follow and whom not.

Rules and regulations are good when carried out. They serve the purpose of improving production and operation and realizing the objectives of the enterprise. Therefore, they must be formulated with great care and enforced rigorously; what they require must be effected and what they prohibit must be stopped. Failure to carry out rules and regulations, their lax enforcement on a case-to-case basis or their hasty changes would lead to the loss of their authority and render them useless. Business management should prevent such a state of affairs when your "soldiers," loyal as they may be, refuse to subject themselves to punishments and the "troops" will not obey your orders because they have never been consistently effected, as was warned by Sun Wu. Necessary changes in the rules and regulations must be made by going through one or another procedure and soliciting the opinions of the people. They must be made public by the department responsible for rules and regulations, or even by the highest leadership of the enterprise.

3. The Employment of Generals

By "general" the military treatise "Sun Zi" means two things. One is commander, or commander-in-chief, as is referred to in the statement: "Now the general is the pillar of the state." (Ch. 3, "The Strategy of Attack") It is referred to as anyone who commands the troops only in a few statements. The other is subordinate or lower-ranking general, as is the case with the statement in Chapter 10, "Terrain": "When the soldiers are strong and their officers weak, there will be laxity in discipline. When the officers are strong and the soldiers weak, there will be collapse of the army. When senior officers are angry and disobedient, and engage the enemy on their own in a resentful state of mind without the commander knowing what they are up to, there will be fiasco." Cao Cao gave his commentary on this: " 'Senior officers' means subordinate generals."

In our case, the word "general" in its broad sense would mean the manager of an enterprise. By analogy, a director of a factory or a manager of an enterprise is in the position of a commander-in-chief, and a section chief or a workshop head is in the position of a subordinate general or a lower-ranking officer. Here, discussing how to employ generals, we will focus on the choice and use of the "subordinate generals."

(A) Choice of Generals.

Able people are the most precious asset of a state. In the Warring States Period (476-221 B.C.) in China's history, King Hui of the State of Wei and King Wei of the State of Chi once set out together for hunting. King Hui asked King Wei whether the state of Chi had any treasures. The latter replied that it had not any. King Hui of the State of Wei said, "A small state as we may be, we have ten bright pearls one 'cun'*. across each which illuminate twelve chariots ahead and behind. How would such a big state as Chi have no treasure at all?" King Wei of the State of Chi replied, "I judge treasures in a way different from Your Majesty's I have an official named Tan Zi who guards the town of Nancheng. Because of him, the state of Chu dares not invade my territory and the twelve princes reigning to the north of the Si River come to pay tribute to me. I have a second official called Bi Zi who is at the head of the garrison of the town of Gaotang. Because of him, people of the State of Zhao cannot take the liberty of fishing on the east bank of my river. I have a third official by the name of Chian Fu who is on garrison duty in the town of Xuzhou. This has led to the people of the State of Yan coming to worship gods at its north gate and the people of the State of Chao coming to worship gods at its west gate and has caused the immigration of over 7,000 households into my State of Chi. I have a fourth official by the name of Zhong Shou who is responsible for theft prevention. Because of him, no one pockets anything found on the road throughout my state. These four officials of mine illuminate a thousand li around with their radiance of flory, to say nothing of mere twelve chariots ahead and behind." And the reply made King Hui of Wei ashamed beyond words. Beside King Wei of Chi who treasured able

---

*About 3.33 cm.—*Trans.*

officials instead of bright pearls, King Hui of Wei could not help feeling his own inferiority.

In China today, able people are also prized by an economic entity such as an enterprise. In the final analysis, competition between enterprises is one for able people. Choice and use of able people are one of the primary duties of a manager and one of the most important criteria for judging of his managerial ability. As Confucius said, "He who recommends a worthy man is even more worthy than the worthy man himself." A worthy director may bring about a new look to his factory, with enhanced efficiency and prosperity. For instance, the Yongle factory of appliances of electric heating in Liwan District of the city of Guangzhou was once reduced to supporting itself by borrowing owing to its mismanagement which had led to low quality of its products, slack business and losses incurred from month to month. By September 1981, the factory had run into a debt of over 60 thousand yuan. As it could do nothing but issue a monthly pay of 20 yuan to each of its workers for subsistence, many workers were ready to leave and find their own way out. At this critical moment, the higher authorities sent to the factory a comrade who was dedicated, full of drive, well-enducated, well-versed in technical know-how and good at working with people. Charged with the technological side of the factory's work, he set about studying what products would suit the needs of the market best and organized their designing and production at once. The factory's work returned to normal just a month later, and the workers were paid in full, plus ten yuan or so in bonus for that month. Three months later, they found their products which sold very well in short supply in many parts of the country. Workers who had left for making a living outside came back one after another. Before long, this comrade was made director of the factory. Using able people without any restraints and perfecting the system of personal responsibility and the system of quality control, he succeeded in raising the quality of products further and winning more and more clients. By early 1984, the products of this factory had gained their market in a dozen or more provinces of the country such as Guangxi, Hunan, Fujian, Hubei, Henan and Yunnan and over 30 cities and counties of Guangdong, the province of its location. Two years passed, and the factory switched from having

60 thousand yuan in debt to having an accumulated fund of 200 thousand yuan, from a monthly pay of 20 yuan per person to an average monthly income of over 100 yuan for each worker. One of the important reasons why this tremendous change took place was the choice and use of right leader and a group of able men. Conversely, the use of a wrong leader in a key position would lead to losses beyond calculation and even ruin of a collective. No wonder the ancients said, "Be precautious about choosing people to appoint," "He who acquires able people will enjoy prosperity; he who loses them will perish," "The key to victory in a war lies in the choice of the right troops," and "The way of commanding troops calls for weighing and balancing which is what choice and use of the worthy people is for." Any manager, of course, wants to get talented and able people for himself. But how can he get them? The ancients also said, "No need to worry about lack of worthy subjects; worry about the absence of the sovereign who is worthy to use them." Able people are everywhere, to be known and chosen and used. Some principles of knowing and using able people offered by the military treatise "Sun Zi" may be of considerable value to business managers.

(1) Choose the Right Person to Cope with a Given Situation and Never Seek Perfect Talents.

A wise manager who has an eye for the able people always selects the right people for the jobs they are competent for respectively and has their efforts well coordinated to ensure the final success of their cause. In 215 A.D., in the Three Kingdoms Period, Sun Quan, sovereign of Wu, led personally his 100-thousand-strong army to attack Hefei garrisoned by 7,000 troops of Wei led by generals Zhang Liao, Yue Jin and Li Dian. The Wei troops were seized with panic. Acting according to his chief commander Cao Cao's instruction that in case Sun Quan should attack the town Zhang and Li were to go into the battle while General Yue was to remain on garrison duty and keep away from the fight, Zhang Liao left Yue Jin at home and charged together with Li Dian and their 800 picked troops into the camps of the enemy before the latter had time to get together. The surprise attack took the wind out of the sails of the Wu army. Having broken through the enemy encirclement, Zhang Liao's troops returned into the town and held their ground, and the people in the town were no more alarmed. Sun Quan's troops besieged the town for a dozen days in vain and withdrew at last. It has been believed that one of the reasons why Hefei did not fall to an overpowering enemy army was that Cao Cao, the chief commander of Wei, knew how to select the right people to cope with the developments in the situation. The knack here was to put people to proper use, taking into account their respective strong points and shortcomings. According to "History of the Three Kingdoms", Zhang Liao "had outstanding prowess", Yue Jin, though "short and small," had courage and insight and, in cooperation with the other two generals, "managed the troops with kindness and never failed to carry out an order or decide on a correct move in time to cope with the enemy," and Li Dian, "a man of heroic disposition", was cooperative in battle and "never scrambled for rewards." By assigning the three generals tasks according to their respective qualities, Cao Cao succeeded in raising the siege.

It should be admitted that any person has his strong points and shortcomings. The use of able people presupposes putting their strong points or their ability to use, rather than seeking perfection in them or ignoring their ability because of their shortcomings. As the ancients taught us, "A talent is valued for his usefulness. Don't demand too much of him." History knows a lot of instances when able men, promoted in disregard of their shortcomings, rendered outstanding service. In the Spring and Autumn Period, Duke Huan of Chi achieved his supremacy over all other feudal princes with the help of Guan Zhong who was no versatile, much less perfect man. He was recommended to the Duke by Bao Shu who knew him very well. Guan Zhong and Bao Shu had run a business in partnership. Sharing out the profits, Guan used to take the better part of them for himself, but Bao never considered him to be greedy, knowing that his friend was very poor and had a family to support. Guan Zhong has offered ideas that proved useless later, but Bao Shu never thought that he lacked wisdom, seeing that it was because he missed the right moment to get things done. Guan Zhong had three times fled the battlefield and the army, but Bao Shu did not take this as the manifestation of his cowardice for he knew that Guan had his old mother to attend to. When Duke Huan of Chi intended to appoint Bao Shu Prime Minister, Bao declined and recommended Guan Zhong for that post instead. The Duke did not feel like it and said, "Guan Zhong had once nearly killed me with an arrow. How could he be made my Prime Minister?" Bao Shu explained, "As a rule, one works for his own sovereign. Guan Zhong had worked then for your brother Prince Jiu who rebelled against you. If only you pardon him now, he will be as loyal to you as he was to Prince Jiu." Duke Huan accepted Bao Shu's advice after careful consideration and appointed Guan Zhong high-ranking minister. Later Guan was made Prime Minister who achieved great order throughout the state of Chi and brought it supremacy over all other feudal states of China in his day. Guan Zhong served under Duke Huan as Prime Minister for as long as 40 years, respectfully called by him "Second Father."

A mathematical expression of Guan Zhong's strong and weak points would look like $7+(-3)$. Bao Shu knew very well Guan Zhong's excellent qualities for running state affairs and so advised Duke of Huan to charge him with heavy responsibility. He put the sum 4, as it were, into the "multiplication operations" of the contention for supremacy by the state of Chi and got the best result. It is a pity, though, that some managers of our enterprises pay little attention to such a simple equation as $7+(-3)=4$, while making appraisal and promotion of their cadres. They can tolerate the negative numbers no more than they can grains of sand in their eyes. They are used to promoting "faultless" people motivated for no accomplishment at all and they seldom select and promote those of real ability and learning who suffer from some defects. The mathematical formula they follow in appointing people is a curious one: $0+0 >7+(-3)$. What they forget is the common knowledge that zero plus zero will always be zero, that zero plus any number will be that number, and zero multiplied by any number will be zero. For the benefit of business management, one should realize that $7+(-3) >0$ and admit the need to judge of a person objectively, to use what he excels in and not to demand of him all that is beyond his ability. This is just what Deng Xucu, Party Secretary of the Shanghai Jiaotong University, has done. It requires courage and insight to promote a person for his strong points in disregard of his weak ones, and this courage and insight can be seen best in a courageous step to promote those able persons who meet with approval and reproach as well. At Shanghai Jiaotong University, the leaders are of the opinion that a person of deeds who shows acuity of wit, devotion to his work and ability to open up new prospects despite differing opinions formed of him is far more preferable than one who shows inability to improve on his work, still less to introduce a new look into the department he is responsible for despite the fact that he has very good relations with high and low alike and no one complain about him. This is what is called "courage and insight"! Commenting on this, an author wrote, "The story reminds me of a saying from an ancient book: 'I would rather be a piece of jade with flaws than a flawless stone' ". Likewise, on the question of making proper use of personnel, I would say, "Use jade with flaws rather than flawless stone."

Since anyone has his strong points to be made use of, can they be used anywhere alike? Of course not. Gu Sixie of the Qing Dynasty (1644-1911) wrote, "A steed may get you through dangers but hardly equals an ox in ploughing; a carriage may transport weights but is hardly as nearly useful as a boat when you are to get across a river." The Russian fable author Krynov wrote, "There will be trouble when the cobbler begins to make pies and the cook to repair shoes." These are metaphors pointing to the importance of the proper use of the right person and the need to let people do what is within their reach, to conform one's ability to his post and to give different posts to people of different abilities, so that everyone has his proper place and room to give his talent a full play. A person with a developed conception of space and abstract things had better be assigned a job in the department of engineering research and development. An optimistic, self-confident, sociable person had better take up sales promotion. A person whose ability for opinion exchanges is not up to much, but whose ability for mathematical calculations is not at all bad, would be competent for financial affairs. A person who is full of enterprising spirit and never content with his daily routine, would be fit for "cracking hard nuts" and pioneering something new. Many factory directors and managers know from their own experience the way to choose, use and train right people. The director of the factory of printing ink in Gangu, Gansu Province, said, "We had a mistaken understanding of the criteria for choosing able men—we emphasized mainly seniority and 'honesty'. And people complained that it was servility, not ability, that counted in our factory. Then we came to realize our mistake and decided to choose and promote able people. But where could they come from? We could not find anyone satisfactory, as we saw above all faults and defects in anyone under discussion. Then we awoke to the truth that the Party's personnel policy demanded of a person both ability and political integrity rather than perfection in every detail. With our horizons widened by the realization, we put forward the principle: 'Essentials come first in judging of one's political integrity, and one skill is enough to prove the worth of one's ability.' By essentials of one's political integrity we mean chiefly one's attitude towards the Party's lines and policies formulated since the Third Plenum of the 11th Congress of the Communist Party of China in 1978 and one's drive for work and personal moral qualities. Stressing one skill of a person, we made it clear that anyone with even a single skill is professionally qualified for a given job. This approach of ours helped to improve our work and bring personal ability into full play so that everyone could do his bit for the common cause."

To make use of one's strong points, a leader must know what strong points to be preferred and what weak points to be forgiven and turned a blind eye to. Of the requirements for a person doing one or another job one or several must be fundamental. Candidates for a job should be qualified by its chief requirements rather than things irrelevant to them. Leaders of the Baiyunshan Pharmaceutical Factory knew this well and acted accordingly. In 1976, the factory, then a small one, could not even keep up payment of wages. Its leaders frequented the personnel department concerned in a vain attempt to get some technicians for the factory. Then someone recommended them a pharmacist, a 1961 graduate from Nanjing Pharmaceutical Institute, who could not put his knowledge and technical know-how to a good use anywhere because of some past faults. The leaders thought the matter out and decided to invite him to work at their factory. Not that they had already a good understanding of the importance of valuing knowledge and esteeming able people; they knew just that the factory could survive and turn out new products only with the presence of good technicians and that the pharmacist's skill was what they needed. Now the leaders made a personal call at the pharmacist's home and came back with him to the factory. They gave him the wages due to him and put him in full charge of the technological work. The middle-aged pharmacist made his all-out effort to start a workshop of injections and improved the factory's work in that same year.

(2) Know a Hero by What He Has Achieved.

There is an old Chinese saying: "A hero need not be one who enjoys success." When it comes to the choice of business managerial workers, however, we cannot but say, "A hero should be one who enjoys success," we must choose successful heroes to make up the backbone of business management. Winning victory in a war is what a general is for, and getting good economic results is what a business magager is meant to do. Winning victory in a war and getting good economic results are ends, and ends are served by means. Means can mean nothing when isolated from the ends. Therefore, conformity of means with ends and unity of motives and results should be taken as the basic guiding principle of using personnel which finds its expression in determining the employment, dismissal, promotion or demotion of managerial workers according to their performance—success or failure in their work.

"To know a hero by what he has achieved" is something different from choosing a leading cadre according to the drive he has shown. The choice of a leading cadre must not be based on the effort he has made, the things he has taken part in and the hardships he has gone through. These may have contributed to his experience, but his appraisal must be based, above all, on the results of his work—how much he has achieved, how much of what is beyond other people's power he has accomplished, and how many things have been done under his leadership and guidance. In short, the merits of a leading cadre are judged by his achievements instead of his efforts, by what he has accomplished rather than what pains he has taken. So a leader who has made no mistakes yet performed no merits has nothing to recommend himself, either, because, he has not really concerned himself with his duty as a leader, and the very failure to perform merits is his mistake, proof of his unworthiness. Admittedly, a man cannot be judged simply by his success or failure in one thing or another at a given moment, because success or failure may be caused by factors other than a man's competence or incompetence, such as time, season and weather, geographical features and other conditions which may affect one's work. But, with the elapse of time and the growing list of cases dealt with, a man is to be finally judged by nothing but his success or failure in his work, for only time proves his worthiness.

"To know a hero by what he has achieved" is also something different from selecting leading workers according to seniority. For the organizational work, seniority may be a very convenient thing by which to judge people's qualification for one or another leading post, while choice of people for it by their performance involves far more inconveniences. But taking seniority as the measure of one's competence will bring untold dangers, for it runs counter to the principle of stressing both ability and political integrity, foster and aggravate the mentality of resting on one's laurels and seeking no more progress, dampen the enthusiasm of many people for forging ahead and thus bring harm to the fundamental interests of the enterprise. In view of all this, many noted enterpreneurs are cautious of the "Seniority first" doctrine in choosing and using people for leading posts. The Sony Company of Japan was said to have burned up all the curriculum vitae of the company's workers and staff members. They hold that managers of a company had better destroy at the bottom of their hearts all the curriculum vitae of its workers and staff members. In China, what we should do is to choose the right people according to their political and educational qualities, their real capability, their performance in the socialist construction and their power for new creations. Of course, we cannot ignore completely one's record of schooling and record of service, as they reflect his educational level and work experience which are of some value for reference. What we disapprove of is the perpetual, oversimplified dominance of educational background and seniority of service in our personnel policy, the stress on what is superficial at the cost of what is essential—one's real ability. We hold that anyone who has been proved possessing real ability in his work can be employed for a leading post regardless of his seniority and diploma, so long as the "Four Cardinal Principles" are adhered to. In the course of the reform of our administrative structure, a lot of enterprises found their practical ways of employing leading cadres. They made the ability to realize the enterprise's guidelines and real talent the criteria for the choice and appraisal of leading cadres and broke all trammels of conventions in promoting enterprising able people. They gave the "number one man" the full right of "forming his cabinet" and obliged him to resign in favour of the more competent one in case he should fail to produce expected results at the expiration of a given term of service. In order to provide the middle-level departments with capable leaders, they appoint abler and younger people as their chiefs and those who had had their seniority built up and had performed some merits yet were less competent as deputies to them.

The practice of these enterprises has led us to the realization that we should not confuse the concept of rewarding according to one's outstanding service and that of assigning a job according to one's ability. Rewards are given on the basis of "merits", and jobs are assigned on the basis of "ability". Rewards involve political honours and material incentives, while jobs mean duties and responsibilities matching abilities. And those worthy of awards and the title of a model worker and capable of innovations and new records for their excellent skills are not necessarily competent for posts of management, much less the ones at higher levels. It is as much a mistake to give those who are incompetent as leaders leading posts as rewards as it is to give intellectuals titles of leading cadres as a sign of respect for their role. When it would be found of greater use to let them work as professionals and make innovations and new records than to give them the responsibility of a leader, they should not be torn away from the jobs they specialize in and made to take up what is beyond their strength. A leading post in a big department would become a load on the mind of, say, a famous mathematician who does not excel at management. Putting one's shortcomings to use in neglect of his strong points would be foolish. Of course, skilled people who have rendered outstanding service or won the title of a model worker may very well shoulder some leading responsibility and there is no lack of such people who are as good at managerial work as at their respective professional work. It is only because some leading comrades confuse the two concepts just mentioned above and assign the wrong persons to leading posts, cutting into the progress of the enterprise as well as the persons thus assigned, that we raise the problem here for all to pay attention to.

(B) Use of Personnel.

(1) Trust the subordinates.

"Sun Zi," ch. 3, "The Strategy of Attack", states, "Now there are three cases in which an army finds itself troubled by the sovereign: When the sovereign commands it to advance, being ignorant that it should not advance, or commands them to retreat, being ignorant that it should not retreat, which is called fettering the army. When the sovereign interferes in the administration of the army, being ignorant of the conditions prevailing in the army, which causes perplexity among officers and men. And when the sovereign meddles in the command of the army, being ignorant of the art of correlating changing circumstances, which makes officers and men suspicious. If the army is perplexed and suspicious, trouble will surely come from the sovereigns of other states. This is called inviting defeat by confusing one's own army."

Likewise, an incorrect approach of a high-ranking business manager towards his subordinates can land his business in trouble. He may take on what ought to be done by his subordinates, showing distrust in them, or interfere in his subordinates' work without knowing them well, or meddle in the exercise of command by his subordinates, ignorant of relevant knowledge and tactics—in short, he dooms himself by denying his subordinates appropriate trust.

Trust put by the leader in his subordinates is quite valuable. Military leaders know well why a general is to be trusted. You don't have to use one whom you distrust, and you don't have to distrust one whom you decide to use. Trust engenders strength. Trust stimulates the enthusiasm of the trusted for work, and their initiative is always proportional to the trust they know. The trust of the leader is the thing that allows the led to bring their talents into full play and work in freedom from any constraints. Only with trust can the subordinates work heart and soul in a common effort with the leaders appreciative of their ability and worthy of their gratitude.

There is a story about how the King of the state of Chin who was to become the First Emperor of the Chin Dynasty (221-206 B.C.) employed and trusted a general. He sent a general named Gan Mao to the state of Wei to reach an agreement with it on a joint attack on the state of Han. With the success of his diplomatic activities, the general sent a messenger to the King, saying that he had better not appoint him commander of the Chin troops meant for the battle. The curious King called Gan Mao to a place named Xirang and asked him why. Gan Mao replied, "Once there was a man in the state of Lu whose name was Zeng Shen, the same as that of one of the noted disciples of Confucius. When that man committed murder, someone told mother of Zeng Shen the disciple of Confucius, 'Your son has killed a man!' She kept on weaving as if nothing had happened. Then a second man came to tell her, 'Your son has killed a man indeed!' She worked on as usual. Then a third man came to say, 'Your son has really killed a man!' The mother then got alarmed, threw away her shuttle, left her loom and escaped by climbing over her wall. Now I am by far inferior to Zeng Shen in ability and moral qualities, and Your Majesty cannot as nearly understand and trust me as Zeng Shen's mother did her son, yet those who are suspicious of me and slander me number more than three. So I fear that Your Majesty may some day throw me away as Zeng Shen's mother did her shuttle." Gan Mao added, "Once Marquis Wen of the state of Wei sent General Yue Yang to attack the state of Zhongshan. Three years later the general returned with success to get his rewards. The marquis showed him a basketful of letters with slanders about him. Yue Yang thanked the sovereign again and again, saying, 'It was solely your support that brought the success of the expedition. My effort was nothing'. Now I am but a guest in the state of Chin. People like Chu Lizi and Gongsun Shuan who have always been dissatisfied with me will probably speak against me on question of the attack on the state of Han, and Your Majesty, I guess, may agree with them." Then the king said, "No, I'll never heed them. I can take a pledge." The king pledged right there, at Kirang. When Gan Mao attacked the city of Yiyang for five months on end without success, Chu Lizi and Gongsun Shuan did speak against him, and the king, influenced by them, was ready to withdraw the troops. Then Gan Mao reminded him, "Remember Kirang!" The king knew what to do and sent reinforcements to the general who finally captured the city, killing 60 thousand enemy troops. Li Zhi, thinker of the Ming Dynasty (1368-1644), commented on this story, "It was no accident that the general could have made his outstanding exploits!" And today the story gives us much food for thought when it comes to the problems of employing and trusting "generals" in business management.

(2) The "sovereign" must not interfere with an able "general". Get the relationship between centralization of power and its decentralization right.

"Sun Zi," ch. 3, "The Strategy of Attack," states, "Now there are five circumstances in which victory can be foreseen: ... He will win whose generals are able and not hampered by the sovereign." The commentary made by Zhang Yu here reads, "A general who is both resourceful and brave should be entrusted with the mission of making war a success and should not be interfered with or checked in his efforts." Generally speaking a leader should vest his subordinates with power and refrain from interfering with their actions, so long as they have the ability to fulfil a certain task and achieve a certain goal independently. Only in this way can suspicion be got rid of and mutual trust between the leaders and their subordinates be promoted.

The principles of avoiding interfering with an able general is also helpful to business management. Konosuke Matsushita, adviser of the Matsushita Electric Industrial Co., Ltd, talked about his principle of management, something similar to the idea of "not interfering with an able general."

Matsushita: "At the corporation, we encourage a deep sense of mission and mutual help. We inspire the enthusiasm for serving the nation with business achievements. Therefore, a maximum decentralization of power is what we need."

"The lower departments can do anything so long as they adhere to the basic guideline of operation and remain mission-conscious. Give them the reins, the freedom from any restraints. Efficiency is boosted in this way."

For any enterprise and any of its departments, Matsushita's idea that "the lower departments can do anything so long as they adhere to the basic guidelines of operation and remain mission-conscious" can also work. It is the same principle as that of not interfering with an able general.

To avoid hampering an able subordinate, the leader should vest them with decision-making power in matters like employment, expenditure and operation. Authorization is often extended by distribution of power. Anyone who manages people faces the problem of authorization and distribution of power. Even if there is but one person under you, you have to consider what to decide on and to do yourself and what to put at his disposal. When management involves few, authorization means nothing but division of labour, but when management involves many in a multilevelled structure with the most miscellaneous jobs to attend to, the manager must, apart from division of labour, handle distribution of power well. Only with the decision-making power distributed to each level of the administration correspondingly can leaders at all levels assume their respective responsibility as they should. The reason is simple: with limited ability, one has to enlist the help of others to do a number of things in different places at the same time. To avoid interfering with an able subordinate is essential for a "divide-and-rule" management by means of authorization and distribution of power and for "doing big things." It means art of leadership without which a manager shows just his incompetence, however occupied he may be.

Wang Zepu, director of the seamless steel tubing mill of the Anshan Iron and Steel Complex, when interviewed by a reporter, said on this score, "You may think I have too heavy a workload on my shoulders, but in reality I have felt myself relaxed since 1980 when I had been director of the mill for one year. If a leader of an enterprise often works from dawn till midnight, that would point to disorder in production. If we demand the workers to fulfil their tasks in an eight-hour workday, why couldn't a factory director and a section chief do so? At our mill, things that can be done in the morning are not allowed to put off until afternoon. A modern enterprise just cannot do without such a strict sequence of work. I demand that everyone fulfil his duty, and in earnest, with succeess."

Without practising the principle of avoiding interfering with an able subordinate, the manager would have to do everything himself, which would lead to his own failure and the suppression of the creativeness of their subordinates and their zeal for work.

As power is something of a variable, authorization and distribution of power will, as a rule, increase, rather than diminish, the power of the manager, if he puts his trust in his subordinates as he should. As is well-known, rational division of labour and effective cooperation can yield a force of "a whole" stronger than the sum of the forces of the separate parts of "the whole". And rational centralization and decentralization of power in management can also bring about "a bigger whole than is expected of the summation of separate parts." Some people know only simple "addition and subtraction" and are untterly ignorant of the knack of "avoiding interfering with the able subordinates," and so they are prone to cling to every bit of their power. Taking the power in their hands as their "private property", they even feel subconsciously that, with each bit of power or authority given and each title or position conferred to someone else, they themselves will lose that much of what is "theirs". Such people are egoistic who believe only in themselves and are always anxious to meddle in everything and take over everything. But among the high-ranking managers they are the least competent and the least "powerful", they are failures.

There are, however, preconditions for "avoiding interfering with the able subordinates." Thus, Konosuke Matsushita said that the lower departments could do anything under the condition that they should adhere to the basic guidelines of operation and remain mission-conscious. In Su Wu's view, a general must not be hampered by his sovereign only when he is able. By "ability" two things are meant here: the skill to do a good job of one's work and the capability to fulfil the tasks assigned by the leadership and realize the set goal with the deepest sense of responsibility and chiefly through one's own effort.

It is also necessary for a manager to remember the following points:

1. One is to be given power according to his ability rather than his position or seniority. It is for the improvement of work that power is given, not for distribution of benefits. Besides, as abilities vary from person to person, authorization should be done on an individual basis, with the ability and educational level of each person in view.

2. To a manager, avoiding interfering with an able subordinate

112

does not mean washing his hands of the business, and authorization does not mean shirking his responsibility. With power distributed to the subordinates, responsibility remains on the shoulders of the leader. A conscientious manager answers for all the problems which occur within the range of his administration, even if his power has been distributed to the lower-ranking officials. He does not interfere with his able subordinates and at the same time gives them support and guidance. Only in this way can the higher and lower levels pull together and make their cause a success.

3. Be sure that power given can be retrieved. Power must not be distributed in excess and at random. Distributing power, the manager should set clearly defined demands and a definite time limit for the fulfilment of a given task and clarify the range of the power distributed. The power given by a manager to his subordinates should not exceed that given to him by his leaders at one level higher. Let a bird fly and keep its flight in the right direction; distribute your power and be sure that you can retrieve it when necessary.

(3) Troops are valued for their quality, not their number.

"Sun Zi," ch. 9, "Marches", states, "An army gains no advantage by sheer numbers. Make no rash advances, be good at concentrating your forces, estimating the enemy conditions correctly and selecting able men, and that is all you have to do." The statement that in war sheer numbers give no advantage is just the same as the popular saying that troops are valued for their quality, not their number. This is a principle for waging wars, and one for employing worthy workers as well. Soon after his ascension on the throne, Li Shimin (559-649 A.D.), or Emperor Taizong of the Tang Dynasty, pointed out, "It is the right choice of the officials, rather than their number, that is valued." He was stressing the officials' quality, not their number.

At present, part of our enterprises employ too many people and indiscriminately. This is due to the small producer's view of some leaders that "the more the workers, the better things can be done" or the inability of others to put excessive hands to use. Modern socialized big production requires that more be done by less people. It is held that one man more in modern big production means one component more in a machine and consequently one more factor of its possible breakdown. In a normal sequence of work, the presence of too many people tends to ruin a cause. Here it is the principle "fewer but better" that works. Where there is plenty of work but a limited number of hands, everyone is heavily loaded, just a bit beyond his ability, and so everyone has to overcome his difficulties and temper himself in the process. This is the very environment in which talents emerge. The principle "fewer but better" means employing a few picked people, and, what is more essential, it also implies that people are even more likely to become capable because of the scarcity of hands. Generally speaking, the concentration of picked people who have already been well trained under one's control is too ideal a situation to be expected. Since among one's sudordinates figures both "jade" and "stone", one has to refine the "jade" and at the same time turn "stone" into "jade" through a kind of tempering. A wise manager knows that the scarcity of hands is the best soil for tapping men's talents. The Shenyang Corporation of Electric Wires and Cables is one of the Chinese enterprises with streamlined administration and high efficiency of work. The Corporation is composed of six specialized enterprises staffed by 13 thousand people. Eight persons work in the Corporation's headquarters made up of its general office and three groups of planning, coordination and consultation, with a clear division of labour and proper cooperation. Each of them does concurrent jobs for several persons. The only gatekeeper, a middle-aged woman, works concurrently as copy clerk, typist, and reception clerk and is charged with the reception and distribution of newspapers and periodicals and the distribution of stationery. And nothing has ever gone amiss. An engineer, concurrently office head, is responsible for surveying the production in the enterprises and gathering information about it. Soon after he took up his post, he made a thorough investigation of over 200 items about all the six enterprises such as the composition of their personnel and the directions in which their products are put to use, and so on. Finding that the Third Electric Wire Factory was falling behind in production, he obliged the relevant groups of the headquarters to help it catch up in management, quality of products and equipment. Only one month passed before the factory succeeded in improving its economic results by a big margin. Success of this Corporation is sufficient testimony of the truth that troops are valued for their quality, not their number.

In China today, quite a few enterprises suffer from overstaffing, which is opposed to the principle "Fewer but better." Our managers should find ways to get rid of the malpractice according to this very principle. At the Laibin Coal Mine in Yunnan Province, the principle "Fewer but better" has been upheld, and diversified production is being conducted by those drawn from the streamlined staff. A brickyard has been set up, with the waste rock from the mine as its raw material, and a cement plant now works on the coal cinder from the mine's power station. Thus, things are made the best use of, and wastes are turned into treasure; people find use for their abilities, and consumers have become producers. Those drawn from the streamlined staff have become an asset for the mine which is now a beehive of activity both on and under the ground. The whole personnel of the mine has taken on a new look, and its economic effectiveness are soaring as never before. A leader of the mine said, "A manager, as I see it, is worthy for his ability to put more people to use on the principle 'Fewer but better', not his ability to discharge them, and for the percentage of the increase of labour productivity and the overall yearly economic results he helps to realize. A manager cannot be considered to have fulfilled his duty unless he can make proper arrangenment for everyone."

Chapter III
Ingenuity in Sales Promotion—a Salient
Point in the Competition for Market

After making estimates and decisions and preparing the enterprise to be invincible by organizational measures taken to better its production, business management comes to grips with sales promotion and competition for market.

Marketing is an essential link in the operation of business. It is the continuation of commodity production, the link between production and consumption and the chief means of distribution of commodities. Failure in marketing would result in the failure to realize the operational objectives of an enterprise and its setback in the heated competition. Unless a product is acknowledged in its circulation by the society with the help of means of sales promotion, the value it embodies cannot be realized, and the productive and operational activities it requires cannot be said to have been finally completed and evaluated. The reason why is that without doing a good job of sales promotion planning and organizational work will yield no results no matter how well they are done, and an excellent sales promotion with the application of certain appropriate stragems will help to make up for the deficiencies in planning and organizational work and bring the best possible results to the business of the enterprise.

Competition puts China's enterprises to severe test in a planned economy supplemented by market regulation. Karl Marx said that marketing was "the salto mortale of the commodity," and "If it falls short, then, although the commodity itself is not harmed, its owner decidedly is." (K. Marx, "Capital," Eng. ed., Moscow, 1959, Vol. I, p. 106) In order not to "be harmed" in the "salto mortale", an enterprise must master the art of marketing and competition.

Competition is a test of strength and that of the skill of sales promotions well. "Sun Zi," ch. 4, "Position", states, "Those skilled in defence hide their forces as under the deepest layers of the subterranean; those skilled in attack move their forces as from above the highest spheres of the firmament. Thus they can both protect themselves and win complete victory." Those engaged in sales promotion had better act in this spirit.

In socialist China, competition is conducted under the guidance of planned economy, within the limits of the policies of the state. Here emphasis is put on socialist morality and fair play in vying for originality and higher quality of products, for better service, lower costs, more reasonable pricing and higher creditability.

"Sun Zi" is a treatise on the law of war. Although contention in war is something different from competition in business, they have something in common after all—they both are a trial of strength to determine supremacy or defeat, and they both involve problems of strategy and tactics and the necessity of knowing oneself and knowing the opponent. In this sense, it is absolutely necessary and practical to study those of military strategy and tactics found useful in the socialist conditions today and apply them to our business management to win victory in competition.

1. Use the Unusual to Win

Conpetition is the contention of products, a kind of close combat on the market, which presents the greatest difficulty for a business manager in the whole process of his work from making plans to selling his product. In his commentary on "Sun Zi," Zhang Yu wrote, "To wrest profit in a direct contention with others is the most difficult thing to do." One of the keys to gaining initiative and victory in such a contention is to "use the irregular." "Sun Zi," ch. 5, "Momentum," states, "When a large army succeeds in withstanding the enemy's attack without suffering defeat, it is the tactical use of the irregular and the regular that makes it possible." "Generally, fighting troops engage with the regular and win with the irregular."* In his commentary on "Sun Zi", Li Quan wrote, "No general can expect to win a contention without irregular or extraordinary manoeuvres."

"To use the irregular to win" means none other than to employ unexpected, vagarious tactics and unusual means to defeat the enemy.

(A) Make Unexpected Moves and Design Unsuspected Schemes.

Unexpected moves and unsuspected schemes are the acme of the art of war. As the ancients said, "The key to victory lies in taking the enemy by surprise and catching him unawares and unprepared." To take into your mind and notice ahead of others the need of the market for one or another product or service, to get a good grip on and a new understanding of what is beneath the notice of others and make something new out of it, to move ahead of others and turn out your fruit of work first—all this bears testimony to what Sun Wu said, "What the ancients called experts of war always conquered an enemy already in the position of the easily conquerable." This is to "use the irregular to win" in business. Equal in judgement and ability with others, you can hardly get the better of them. In Chapter 4, "Position," of his treatise, Sun Wu wrote his brilliant argument as follows:

"To foresee a victory with the wisdom of the ordinary man is not the acme of excellence, nor is it the acme of excellence to come off victorious through bitter fighting and so to be acclaimed "Excellent" everywhere under Heaven. For lifting an autumn hair shows no great strength; seeing the sun and the moon is no proof of the sharpness of sight; hearing the thunderclap bears no testimony to acuteness of hearing. What the ancients called experts of war always conquered an enemy already in the position of the easily conquerable." In this way the author pointed out that the acme of skill is to know what others do not know and to win by means known to none and that, to

---

*In the terminology of the military science of ancient China, the regular suggests garrison forces, forces clamping down on the enemy, frontal attack, overt attack, and fighting in accordance with normal principles, while the irregular implies manoeuvring forces, forces attacking by surprise, roundabout attack, covert surprise attack, fighting in some ingenius, extraordinary ways as required by the circumstances.—*Trans.*

conquer easily, one must first create appropriate conditions. Therefore, a skilled manager should have a special insight to see what is hardly noticeable for now and move ahead of others to win victory.

Having read news reports about road accidents caused by motorcylists, a manager of a big department store lost no time in securing one thousand helmets for motorcyclists. Less than a month had passed after that before the communications authorities declared ban on motorcycling without wearing a helmet. And the store did a great business, as its helmets were sold out instantly. The manager owed his success to his ability to discern a small clue and take timely steps.

While the transistorization of radio was going on all over the world, Japan's Sony Corporation purchased the patent right on integrated circuit from the United States and was the first to apply the new technology to the miniaturization of radio sets. This move ahead of others was naturally followed by success.

(B) Use Unique Skills and Extraordinary Tricks Which Are Beyond Others.

He who is good at using the irregular does what others cannot do or fail to do. He uses his unique skills and extraordinary tricks to help his enterprise win victory in the competition just as new weapons help win a war. Whoever has his unique skills ready is most likely to enjoy the freedom of survival and growth.

An extraordinary advertisement can bring amazing result. In the United States, of every three watches sold one has the brand mark of "Timex," and in Europe and Africa "Timex" watches have brought drastic change in the market in favour of their manufacturer. Why is it so? One reason is that the "Timex" watches are priced extraordinarily low; they are low-grade watches well-known all over the world. In 1950, the retail price of a "Timex" for men ranged from 6.95 to 7.95 dollars, and that in 1954 was $12.95. In 1958, the first batch of complete sets of "Timex" watches for women—one for the dressing room, another for the court, still another for general purposes—sold for less than $50 per set. These low-priced watches became popular articles of daily use and gifts for the occasion of Christmas, the New Year, graduation from a school or the birthday of father or mother. The Timex Company claimed in the 1960s that it had taken over 36 percent of the market of watches for women priced under $50 each. Another reason for Timex's success is that the way it promoted its sales and advertised on TV was amazingly attractive. As was reported by the press, Timex promoted its sales in much the same way as a circus attracts its spectators, which was totally new to the conservative watch sellers. Visiting a watch shop, the Timex salesman would crash one of his watches against the wall or throw it into a bucket of water to show its shockproof and waterproof qualities. Thus, the Timex Company acquired its great reputation for such "flogging experiment." On TV Timex showed how a Timex watch continued to work well after it had been dragged on the tail of a galloping horse, or thrown from a height of 135 feet, or tied to a racing surf-board or amphibian.

This "flogging" advertisement brought success to Timex everywhere. Thanks to its propaganda campaigns, Timex, still little known in Africa in 1962, sold 10 thousand of its watches in that continent in December 1963 alone. The same trick of advertisement enabled Timex to enter the French market soon after that and by the mid-1960s Timex was ready to take over the West German market of watches. Similarly, in order to win market in Australia, the Japanese manufacturers of the watches of the brand "Citizen" went out of their way to throw the watches down from a flying helicopter to a designated square for anyone to pick up for himself. This created quite a stir. Thousands of people crowding the square saw for themselves how watches from the sky landed intact. And the story carried the fame of the "Citizen" watches far and wide.

One more examples of unique ways of successful advertisement. Scores of years ago, there was a Liangxinji toothbrush shop in Shanghai which solicited customers by putting an advertisement of artistic exaggeration in the newspaper. It was a picture showing a man pulling the bristles off a toothbrush with a pair of pincers, pulling with might and main, but in vain. And the caption read, "Not a single bristle to be pulled off."* This unique yet humorous advertisement made the Liangxinji toothbrush famous at once for its high quality— "not a single bristle to be

---

*A pun on a Chinese idiom meaning "to be reluctant to part with a single coin."—*Trans.*

pulled off."

Extraordinary service brings extraordinary reputation. The Hengdeli ("Prosperity") watch and clock store in Tianjin had a brisk business because of the extraordinary accuracy of its watches and clocks. Each batch of watches or clocks it was stocked with had to go one by one through the most careful quality test made by a most skilful master worker. Those failing to keep good time were resold, to avoid their appearance in this store. The customers were attracted by the great variety of watches and clocks on display on the walls or in the glass cabinets and amazed, on a second glance, by the way their hands pointed to the same place —literally to-a-second standard of accuracy! This was a most fascinating advertisement in itself, something "original" then admired by yet inaccessible to the store's counterparts in the country.

Extraordinary quality wins an extraordinary position for a product. The Maotai wine produced in China's Guizhou Province owes its world renown to its unique fragrance. A story has been told about how at a world liquor appraisal meeting samplers from many countries of the world disdained China's Maotai wine for its poor package. They were astounded by its strong fragrance when a Chinese selesman, hitting upon an idea, deliberately dropped one bottle of the wine and crashed it to pieces. Thus the Maotai wine burst into fame, ranked as one of the world's most celebrated wine. Two "bat" brand electric fans produced by the Changjiang machinery plant of Nanjing on display in the showcase of the Xinjiekou department store in that city operated 20,760 hours on end and, when taken apart for examination, they proved up to the standards set by the state all the same. So the "bat" brand fans became known as "longevity fans."

A unique marketing policy yields satisfactory results. Up to 1980, the east Zhejiang knitwear factory, like many other factories of the country, had its products purchased and sold solely by the commercial authorities in a planned way. In 1981, a system of purchase by choice through sampling was introduced, which put the factory before the test of competition. The factory leaders then pooled their wisdom to find a way out, inviting the orders from the commercial departments, companies, clothing factories, production brigades and individual operators of other localities while working hard toward the planned purchase of its products by the local commercial authorities. They treated the customers from other localities just as warmly as they did the local commercial authorities, trying to avoid dependence of the factory's business on the local purchasing station, or one given area, business point or shop alone. They sold their products in a great number of shops scattered in a large area, depending on a good reputation and wide relations with customers. As a result, the factory did very well at a time when knitwear was dull of sale throughout the country.

A surprising pledge causes an extraordinary reaction. In 1982, the Yunnan chemical engineering fittings plant sent a detachment of workers outside to contract for the installment of mechanical and electrical equipment. The detachment found in the business talks with the Longling County sugar refinery that the refinery had not much faith in the capability of the workers from a fittings plant for installment of equipment. Although the workers of the fittings plant were all from the former Yunnan chemical engineering installment brigade and could very well satisfy the technological requirements of the sugar refinery for the installment of its equipment, the refinery leaders hesitated to place their full confidence in the workers who had never installed sugar refinery equipment and sign the contract. At this critical moment, the fittings plant negotiators offered a surprising promise: In case the installment work should fail to meet the technological requirements and ensure the start of the refinery's work as scheduled, the fittings factory would voluntarily pay a fine of 10 thousand yuan for each day's postponement and 20 thousand yuan for each day's postponement four days after that. This decisive move scattered the other party's doubts much as a gust of wind would do the clouds, and the contract was signed at once. The installment was finished five days ahead of schedule, and the first test run proved a success to the satisfaction of both parties. From then on, the fittings plant did good business everywhere with the help of its extraordinary pledge.

(C) Change Your Tactics in an Endless Variety.

As has been stated, to use the irregular to win means to use the schemes unknown to others to win victories. And such extraordinary schemes spring from a creative mind. Life has shown that whoever racks his brains to study problems can offer original schemes. This was expounded over 2,000 years ago by Sun Wu who believed that the most ordinary and the most fundamental could yield endless, unbelievable new things, if thought over, utilized and changed. In Chapter 5, "Momentum," of his treatise, Sun Wu wrote, "Now those who excel in producing the irregular do so in ways as endless as Heaven and Earth and as inexhaustible as the torrent of the great rivers.... The musical notes are only five in number but, combined in various ways, they produce so many melodies that one can never hear them all. The basic colours are only five in number but, combined in various ways, they produce so many hues that one can never see them all. The tastes are only five in number but, combined in various ways, they produce so many flavours that one can never taste them all. The lines of waging war are only two: the regular and the irregular, but, combined in various ways, the regular and the irregular produce so many manoeuvres that one can never know them all." This statement on the use of the irregular is itself a piece of original writing with its ideas, arguments, style and figures of speech all being extraordinary. It shows figuratively the truth that there is no end to the irregular in dealing with the endless changes, that the extraordinary comes from the ordinary and those who are capable of the extraordinary are skilled at but using the ordinary better, in an extraordinary way. Thus, the basic music notes are put into various melodies—those just so-so, those inferior or those superior. Likewise, the basic colours and flavours used by different people can produce the most different results. This statement of Sun Wu's also teaches that those good at using the irregular never repeat their tactics in accommodation to the never-ending changes of the circumstances. Creative thinkers were dreamers. Dreams come from diffusive thinking, a process consisting of supposition, imagination and creation. In the recent years the Haiyan shirt factory of Zhejiang Province has been developing with one innovation after another, guided by the idea that it should produce what others cannot, create what is new to others and turn to a new path far away from the craze others follow. In April 1980, factory director Bu Xinsheng learned in Shanghai that a polyester fibre knitwear dress material with a new design of red flowers on a black background was very popular with young women, and the factory lost no time in putting out batches of women's shirts of that material and putting them on the market. Very soon such shirts nicknamed "black peony" came into fashion in all big cities of the country. Realizing then that the coming of the high tide in sales would be the very beginning of the low tide in production, the factory leaders decided resolutely to stop the production of the "black peony" in June 1983 and switch to new products such as women's shirts with an upright soft collar and lace trimmings. By the latter half of 1983, it was the turn of these new shirts to be in vogue on the market. This was how the Haiyan shirt factory produced something new and extraordinary from time to time to keep itself ahead of other shirt factories.

There are managers, however, who are content with the conventional ways and are used to following crazes by putting out what sells well on the market for the moment, instead of striving for opening up new paths with the extraordinary. Such a practice may be convenient, but is unwise, because in days of relative stability of the market it brings limited profits, though it involves little risks, but in times of drastic changes on the market, it may ruin an enterprise, as the resources put into a certain production have no time to be turned into a productive force before it turns obsolete. Qi Baishi, great master of traditional Chinese painting, warned, "Those who mimic me will perish!" urging painters to create new things instead of imitating others. Between 1980 and 1983 there was a rush among some factories in some provinces and municipalities to start the production of bicycles, watches and sewing machines, but problems cropping up landed their producers in a dilemma afterwards. The trouble lay in the very fact that they knew nothing but follow a craze. Others would hold on to their old products, claiming that it is their honour to "maintain old traditions." Managers like these tend to concentrate on maintaining what has already been achieved and, when their old ways prove a failure, they would argue it off, "It has always been so," or "Former managers did it always this way", or "I've always kept to our traditions; there's no novelty from me." Yes, the trouble lies just in the lack of novelties. Shang Yang, (c. 390-338 B.C.), noted reformist in Chinese history, wrote on this score: "The ordinary people are used to traditions, and the scholars are confined to what they have learned;" "The sages refuse to follow traditions of the old, if only this will help to make the state strong."

Things are, however, of a dual nature. Skilful use of the irregular can bring big profits, but awkward employment of it without a careful consideration would land one in trouble. Therefore, it might be of some help to pay due attention to the following points while you try to "use the irregular" to win:

(1) Risks Involved.

Both the regular and the irregular, as a rule, are employed in war. In business management, the regular meaning keeping to the conventional and the irregular meaning innovation and creation must be employed properly, each as the occasion would dictate, or in combination with each other. The use of the irregular may lead to remarkable success, as when a new product is welcomed on the market, or end up with a fiasco, and success and fiasco can be only just one step apart. Why is it so? Because the use of the irregular is often accompanied by risks, as in the cases of Han Xin's forming the ranks of his troops before the river, Zhuge Liang's empty-city stratagem bluffing the enemy by opening the gates of a weakly defended city, and Deng Ai's (197-264 A.D.) surprise attack by taking the dangerous path of Yinping. Statistics shows that only an average of around 30 percent of the new products can be accepted by the users and bring their manufacturers profits. Therefore, a manager cannot be too careful in trying to win with their new products. He must do his best to avoid making a fruitless decision or devising a plan for nothing. Trial production and trial sales would give him a correct understanding of his external and internal environment, as has been discussed in Chapter One of this book.

(2) Relatedness of Things and Continuity of Development.

Things are related to each other; the regular and the irregular complement each other. So, firstly, using the irregular to win, one has to take into consideration all the relevant conditions. In the past years of adjustment of the national economy, a certain leading department issued a directive to the enterprises under its control, saying, "Find ways to make business lively. You can do everything in the field of your specialty." The words "in the field of your specialty" indicated that the actions to be taken must be related to the specialty of the enterprise and not be divorced from it. Thus, a chemical production machinery works that needs to operate at only a percentage of capacity to fulfil its tasks may start on diversification of its business. This is correct in principle, yet it should remember the special features of the trade it belongs to—chemical production machinary, and those of the works itself. Only in that case can the enterprise "use the irregular" instead of "doing it in a queer way"; only in that case can the enterprise maintain its links with the leading and the subordinate onganizations by utilizing the resources, the production conditions, the production experience and the marketing channels of the department it belongs to. Otherwise, the pursuit of "the irregular" and "the novel" would deprive the works of the support of other organizations, and it would take even greater risks, operating in isolation.

Secondly, strong points and weak points are related to each other, and neither should be ignored. This is because the "use of the irregular" and the "creation of novelty" is a continually employed tactical means rather than a makeshift device. Manager of the "Nanfang Building" Department Store Deng Hanguang used to remind his salesmen and staff workers, "Reputation of our store is much more valuable than a fixed asset of millions of dollars." Once it was found that a batch of the store's TV sets which sold very well had important parts of an inferior brand. The manager decided immediately to stop selling them. Someone suggested to sell the whole batch out—"Just this once!" But the manager refused to do so—"Not even once can we afford to do such a foolish things as to ruin our own reputation." In a striking contrast, a factory of electric blankets in a certain county advertised its products on TV again and again, asserting that their quality was of top grade and it offered the best service, but in reality it let the customers down with its low-quality products and deserved no credit at all for violating contracts. The factory managers never expected that they lifted the huge stone of harming people to benefit themselves only to drop it on their own feet. At the mere mention of that factory's products, people now know how to "keep a respectful distance" from them. This is just a case of what our farmers put it, "If a man fools the earth, it will in turn fool his belly." In business management, the use of the irregular should stay free from any hint of deception; what is needed here is honesty and scientific approach and a backing of strength. A sober-minded manager would never agree to a "get-rich-quick-and-get-away-with-it" approach.

Thirdly, "the irregular" may some day turn into "the regular", and an "original" scheme will be employed by all. Therefore a manager should vary his original schemes from time to time. Thus, when a certain product of yours makes its first appearance on the market, you can win for its novelty; when it ceases to be something new, you can win for its top quality; and when such a high-quality product is made throughout the country, you can win for its cheapness and your extraordinarily good service.

2. "He Who Knows the Art of Using the Devious and the Direct Will Win"

The manager of an enterprise is not just the director of today, but chiefly the planner of tomorrow. As an old Chinese saying goes, "The far-sighted sees a thing before its budding, and the wise avoids a danger before it takes shape." A wise man has foresight and sagacity and takes precautions against trouble when it is still nowhere to be seen. In the competition for market, the first and foremost thing is to fix long-term objectives and devise long-term plans directing the development of the business. And short-term plans are to be made under the guidance of the long-term ones. Our forebears said, "He who lacks a long view is doomed to immediate trouble." They also said, "Petty minds mature quickly, and great minds mature slowly." All this is equally true of business. The manager of a modern industrial enterprise must have foresight and sagacity in order to keep his orientation and remain invincible by providing against possible trouble in competition. And one of the important methods of thinking useful for a sagacious manager is to "know the art of using the direct and the devious."

"Sun Zi", ch. 7, "Contention for Advantages," states: "The difficulty of contending for advantages lies in making the devious the direct and to turning trouble into advantage," "He who knows the art of using the devious and the direct will win". If "to wrest profit in a direct contention with others is the most difficult thing to do," to "know the art of using the devious and the direct" is even more difficult. One who knows how to handle the relationship between the direct and the devious approach will be victorious and "one who does not know how to make the devious the direct and to turn trouble into advantage cannnot contend with the enemy for gains," as is pointed out by Chen Gao in his commentary on "Sun Zi". "To make the devious the direct" means to take a roundabout path in order to create necessary conditions for gaining victory more directly, effectively and quickly. "Sun Zi", ch. 7, "Contention for Advantages", states, "One who deliberately takes a devious route, diverts the enemy with a bait and thus arrives before him though sets out after he does knows the art of using the devious and the direct." The essence and the meaning of the art to make the devious route the direct one could not be shown clearer by these words. Mr. Mulayama, a Japanese expert working in China, discussing the application of the theses of "Sun Zi" to business management, said that the 25,000-li Long March made by the Chinese Red Army in the 1930s was the first instance of "Making the devious the direst" offered by the Chinese Communist Party. The Long March was caused by the mistakes of the Party's leaders, which was, of course, a bad thing, but the completion of the Long March under a new Party leadership turned a bad thing into a good one. The second of such instances was the abstention from killing Chiang Kai-shek in the 1936 Sian Incident, which meant sacrifice of the immediate gains in favour of a victory of the War Against Japanese Aggression. The third instance was the abandoning of Yenan and some other cities of the Liberated Areas in 1946-1947, which quickened the liberation of the whole country. And the economic readjustment under way in today's China, according to Mr. Mulayama, is still another instance of "making the devious the direct", viewed from the angle of the overall situation and China's long-term interests.

In our view, studying the art of "making the devious the direct", one should first of all understand that *the devious contains the direct and the direct yields the devious.* This was explained by V. I. Lenin when he wrote, "Human knowledge is not (or does not follow) a straight line, but a curve, which endlessly approximates a series of circles, a spiral. Any fragment, segment, section of this curve can be transformed (transformed one-sidedly) into an independent, complete, straight line, which then (if one does not see the wood for the trees) leads into the quagmire, into clerical obscurantism (where it is anchored by the class interests of the ruling classes)." (V. I. Lenin, Collected Works, Eng. ed., Foreign Languages Publishing House, Moscow, 1961, V. 38, p. 363)

Business management knows plenty of instances testifying to this truth. Thus, in order to make short-term, medium-term or long-term operational plans, the enterprise employs a large number of its staff members and draws on big sums of its funds for gathering relevant data. This is a job following a zigzag and roundabout path. Instead of circling endlessly around a ready-made plan, it is a spiralling movement bringing one's level of cognition upward and plans to perfection. The more seriously and effectively this job is done, the surer will be the success of plans. Sometimes an enterprise may find the product it has sold sent back by the customer, which is, of course, a setback for it. A wise manager would always receive the customer cordially and undertake to replace the product not up to standards. He knows that "the devious contains the direct," and a bad thing can be turned into a good thing, that mishandling this matter will mean the loss of not only the faith of a customer in the enterprise but also its credit in general. A wise manager would always do his best to remedy the slip and make up for the loss of the customer so as to satisfy him and "get the devious nearer to the direct" for the enterprise.

Ancient merchants and modern entrepreneurs in China have known many knacks of "making the devious the direct," and some of them have been crystallized in proverbs and maxims, such as "Less profit this year makes for more gains next year;" "Get a new product on its feet and see it off for some distance; deliver it to the very doorsteps of the customers;" "Better to bustle around for the profit of one cent than to sit idle waiting for the profit of two cents;" "Expect a 30-percent profit, and you can live on your profit; expect a 70-percent profit, and you will live on your capital." The experienced operators know well that "small profits but quick turnover" is the best stratagem. The last two maxims listed here may serve as the best illustration of the art of using the devious and the direct. Thus, of the two shops selling deep-fried dough cakes, shop A uses one catty of oil for frying six catties of dough and shop B uses the same amount of oil for frying five catties of dough, and they sell them at the same price. It may seem that shop A gains more profits than shop B does. In fact, it is shop B that is wiser, because more oil goes into each of its cakes and this makes them more crisp and tasteful and so brings more buyers. In contrast, shop A attracts fewer or even no buyers. And then shop B gains more profit by selling more at a lower profit rate, just the case as Sun Wu wrote about in his military treatise: "One who deliberately takes a devious route, diverts the enemy with a bait and thus arrives before him though sets out after he does knows the art of using the devious and the direct." The Limin Confectionery in Tianjin produced chocolate pellets in cardboard packages of 24 each. They sold for 0.27 yuan apiece, and one ton of them brought a profit of 2,000 yuan. But only 30 tons were sold per year, which netted a total profit of 60 thousand yuan. Beginning from 1982, the confectionery has offered its product in plastic bags of 25 pellets each at a price of 0.19 yuan, getting a profit of only over 800 yuan per ton. A simple calculation would seem to show the confectionery operating at a loss. But, because of the simplified packing, the yearly sale of the product has soared to 250 tons netting a profit of 210 thousand yuan, an increase of 250 percent.

The second aspect of the art of "making the devious the direct" consists of the ability to "foresee what is near and what is far away" and to "move according to the knowledge of what is light and what is weighty". A leather shoe factory of country A and a leather shoe factory of country B, for example, each sent a salesman of its own to an island in the Pacific Ocean to find there market for its products. On the first day after their arrival on the island, the two salesmen sent their respective telegrams home, the one to country A reading, "No one on this island wears any leather shoes; I'll fly home on the first plane tomorrow," and the one to country B reading, "Very good. I'll stay here. No one here wears shoes." Soon after that the leather shoe factory of country A closed down, but that of country B made a fortune. The reason was that the two salesmen took different views on the question, that of country A seeing only the surface of things, but that of country B seeing the potential needs of the islanders for shoes and consequently the potential purchasing power and a market to be monopolized. Early in this century, a chief manager of the Bell Telephone Company of the United States, helped with his foresight and wisdom make his company one of the fastest growing big enterprises of the world. His four successful policies enabled the Bell Company to survive and develop and grow fast amidst all kinds of hazards. Firstly, he raised the slogan that service is Bell's aim; secondly, he introduced the so-called "public control"; thirdly, he set up the Bell Institute; and fourthly, he devised a "public funding market". All these four decisions were not aimed at meeting the immediate needs of the moment; they were major creative decisions of strategic importance for the future. Contrary to the well-known views of the time, they became the focus of controversies, and the chief manager himself was dismissed by the company's board of directors. But some years later, the four decisions turned out to be the best remedies for the troubles the company was faced with and brought it tremendous success. At that time, as good service became the key to the development of an enterprise, the slogan that "Service is Bell's aim and the measures taken for improving its service and the standards set for it enabled the Bell Company to meet the demands of the public. As the U.S. Government prepared to nationalize the telephone enterprises, the "public control" introduced to ensure the interests of the public kept the Bell Company on its feet. As the rapid progress of science and technology had contributed to the significant development of telecommunications, the telecommunications technology first introduced by the Bell Institute pioneered the new developments of science and technology of the time. The U.S. funding market was then turning from the speculators' market of the 1920s to the market of the middle-class housewives, market of "Aunt Sally," and so the public funding market catered to the wishes of "Aunt Sally" to be free from risks, to have ensured dividends, to enjoy increase of assets and to be free from the threats of inflation. This enabled the Bell Company to secure an ample supply of funds in the recent 50 years.

A manager should also know that "the direct can yield the devious". If an enterprise's product C, low-quality and low-priced, sells well, and its product A, high-quality and high-priced, and product B of a middle grade find insignificant market, the wise manager would not only take pains to promote the sales of products A and B but also worry about the growing popularity of product C for fear that the excessively long stay on the market and high popularity of the low-grade product C would distort the producer's image, leaving the customers with the impression that his enterprise offers only low-quality, low-priced products. His worry is not without reason, for product C is but a small section, a fragment, of the spiralling curve of the enterprise's development and, if this small section is made an independent straight line growing in length without changing its direction in time, it would lead people who "do not see the wood for the trees" "into the quagmire", as V. I. Lenin pointed out. As the brisk business with product C implies the truth that "the direct can yield the devious", the manager must put its production and marketing under control and adjust them at an appropriate moment, to prevent the direct, "straight line" of product C from leading the enterprise "into the quagmire". Take the Changzhou tractor plant which manufactures Dongfeng-12 brand walking tractors. In 1980, in the keen competition between the country's agricultural machinery plants for market, this plant was faced with the problem of how to keep its existing market and open up a new one. Of the various alternatives of marketing stratagems offered in the plant one was to cut down the price by a big margin. Its advocates stressed that all other plants were using price-cut as a means of competition to set off the Changzhou tractor plant's superiority in the quality of products. They suggested that the Changzhou plant reinforce its superiority in the quality of products with a competitive price-cut so as to make itself unmatched on the market, forcing the smaller tractor plants suffering losses to withdraw from competition, switch to other business and make way for the Changzhou plant. But the leaders of the Changzhou tractor plant declined this suggestion, seeing "the devious" in "the direct" consisting in a drastic price-cut aimed at seizing market. They feared that such a price-cut might spoil the plant's reputation, as it might create a misleading impression that its products could hardly find a buyer, and it would ruin the plant's long-sustained popularity among the small enterprises of the same trade which it had always lent a helping hand. In addition, to squeeze others out with a drastic price-cut would run counter to the principles of socialist competition. Finally, they came to the policy of making full use of the plant's superiority, stressing real effectiveness of sales promotion and enhancing the plant's competing capability, which called for the further improvement of the quality of their famous-brand products by allocating more funds for them, the adoption of various means of sales promotion and channels of marketing according to the market conditions, and the enhancement of the use value of the products which would mean more real benefit to their users. This new policy yielded quick results—the original market was kept intact without a price-cut, and a new market covering the provinces of Anhui, Fujian, Guangdong, Gansu and Shaanxi was gained without putting any advertisements in the press. In 1980 and 1981, when the total sales volume of the walking tractors of the country dropped, the Changzhou tractor plant had its own sales volume increased. Facts showed that their policy of development without a price-cut was successful, a policy resulting from the realization that "the devious" that "the direct" could yield should be avoided.

The manager's art of using the devious and the direct and his knowledge of "the light and the weighty" only lay the foundation of the development of his enterprise. He has to create conditions for turning "the devious" into "the near direct" and to transform contradictions in the direction favourable to his business. Such conditions should be understood thoroughly and created in good time to turn "the devious" into "the near direct" and trouble into advantage. The following table shows the possibility of transforming "the devious" or trouble into "the direct" or advantage:

Table Three

Stage of Business Activity	"The Devious" or Trouble	Conditions for Finding a Way Out	Purpose of Work
Planning	Products unsuitable to the needs of the market	To make it clear what the social needs are and what products and services the enterprise can offer the society	To turn out products needed by the market
Production	Production organization in a bad way; failure to use resources effectively and to give full play to the workers' initiative.	To organize efficient production and improve production management; to satisfy the needs of the workers to enhance their drive for work	To effect the best organization of production to offer the society the products and services needed
Marketing	Reluctance of customers to buy the products or their failure to buy them at present	To employ various effective means of marketing	To satisfy the needs of both the society and the enterprise

3. "There Are Commands of the Sovereign Not to Be Obeyed"

"Sun Zi", ch. 8, "Endless Tactical Adaptations", states, "There are commands of the sovereign not to be obeyed." This occurs on special occasions, one of which is when a general is in operation, far away from the sovereign.

There is a story in the famous historical novel "The Romance of the Three Kingdoms" telling of Sima Yi killing Meng Da. When Zhuge Liang prepared to undertake an expedition against the Kingdom of Wei, Meng Da, a general of the Kingdom of Shu who had surrendered to Wei, intended to capture Loyang, the capital of Wei, with his troops stationed at the three cities of Jincheng, Xincheng and Shangyong, and turn over back to Shu with the success of such a great exploit as a tribute. Zhuge Liang was sure that if Meng rebelled Wei in a hurry, he would be captured by Sima Yi, then a commander and governor of Wei, so he wrote Meng a letter, saying, "Be on the alert and prepared against any event. Don't take it lightly". But Meng Da thought that since Sima Yi had his headquarters in Wancheng, about 800 li away from Wei's capital, he would have to ask his sovereign for instruction even if he got wind of his preparations for the rebellion, and it would take one month for the imperial instruction to reach Sima Yi at a time when the rebellion would have been ready to start. So, thinking little of Zhuge Liang's warning, Meng said, "Zhuge Liang is said to be overcautious. From this matter I can see it is true." On hearing of Meng Da's intention to rebel, Sima Yi decided to dispatch his troops against him at once. His elder son reminded him that he would have to send an urgent message to the emperor about this. He replied, "It would take as long as one month for the message to go to His Majesty and the imperial decree to come here, and it would be too late". So the rebellion ended up with Meng Da's death. The story tells us that Sima Yi successfully employed two principles for military actions. One of them was: "act first and report afterwards," "A general in operation need not obey all the commands of the sovereign". Although normally an imperial decree should first be available for a military action, emergencies required that an immediate decision be made and an instant action taken to cope with the situation. The other principle was to take the unprepared enemy by surprise, which brought death to Meng Da.

An episode in the film "Dong Cunrui" illustrates the same thing. The enemy did not attack the position of the group Dong Cunrui belonged to, but assaulted its flank positions in waves, and they were in great danger. Dong suggested to the group leader to attack the enemy in coordination with the flanks, but the group leader insisted on waiting for order from above. So they quarrelled, and Dong charged forward on his own. The battle finished, Dong thought that he had violated discipline, but, to his surprise, was cited for it. It can be seen that special circumstances do occur in military actions, and mechanical observation of discipline must give way to flexibility when necessary.

The two theses of "Sun Zi"—"There are commands of the sovereign not to be obeyed," and "He will win whose generals are able and not hampered by the sovereign"—are principles for handling the relations between the commander and his subordinates. The latter is for the manager to coordinate with his subordinates so that their initiative and creativeness can be brought into full play, while the former is his guide to handling the relations with his own leader, not necessarily the sovereign, in a special situation.

The military tenet that there are commands of the sovereign not to be obeyed has created many a hero in history; it also has ruined those who acted arbitrarily without a proper knowledge of the overall situation or fell under the fire of jealousy and enjoyed no appreciation by the sovereigns. Today, this tenet can be of great importance to business management, and to the decision on competition tactics in particular.

China is a vast country with a multitude of various enterprises, a condition fovourable for building up the nation's strength. But no guideline or policy of the government can cover the specific conditions of all the localities of the country and offer the measures and methods of work suited to all our enterprises. The managers of an enterprise should know how to deal with the particularity of things in order to find out their essence and the law governing their changes and avoid being content with a general knowledge and conducting stereotyped guidance of work with no breakthrough or innovation in prospect. An enterprise should be good at taking particular measures to deal with things particular under the guidance of the basic tenets of Marxism and the Party's general policy. Proceeding from reality, it can have a free hand in undertaking anything beneficial to the cause of the nation.

(A) "When You See the Correct Course, Act; Do Not Wait for Orders".

Zhang Yu's commentary on Sun Wu's statement: "There are commands of the sovereign not to be obeyed" reads, "*When you see the correct course, act; do not wait for orders."* This is to say that so long as an action is dictated by the actual circumstances, corresponds with appropriate norms and helps realize the expected results most efficiently, it can be taken without waiting for sanction. This was just the case with Sima Yi vanquishing Meng Da's rebellion, as has been mentioned above. Modern management science holds that the nearer the place where a decision is made to the place where the problem is to be tackled, the better, and the farther the former is away from the latter, the worse. A problem solved in time guarantees the best economic results. In case an enterprise should come across a problem to be decided on by the organization which is its leader or even by the ministry or commission concerned of the central government, yet time cannot wait until you go through all the formalities, and opportunity cannot afford to be missed, bold decisions should be made and actions taken to seize the moment with a deep sense of responsibility so as to ensure your success.

In the fourth quarter of 1981, the Yunnan chemical engineering fittings plant had to make an important decision. At that time, the plant was responsible for the installation of equipment in the Longling County sugar refinery which, according to the contract, was to go into operation on March 1, 1982. If a delay should occur because of poor quality of installation work or for some other reasons, the plant would be fined 10 thousand yuan for each day's delay; if the installation should be completed ahead of schedule, it would be rewarded with one thousand yuan for each day saved. As the refinery failed to complete the construction of its factory building as was scheduled and provide the fittings plant with all the necessary blueprints for the installation of equipment as was provided for in the appendix to the contract, the plant had the right to postpone the date of completion of its work free from the responsibility for any losses incurred. But, to ensure the start of the refinery's operation on March 1, the local farmers had already planted their sugarcanes in time, and the date of getting in the sugarcane harvest could not be put off, otherwise the sugarcanes cut and stacked for too long would be reduced to dried faggots. Thus the problem of how to complete the project by March 1 with a shortened time limit became the major concern of both the refinery and the plant. The plant worked at full capacity at that time and could send no more people for the jobs at the refinery. And the installation brigade could not fulfil its tasks in time unless everyone worked overtime for at least five days a week beginning from November 21. Then problems would ensue: how to keep the workers safe and healthy when they all work overtime for so many months on end? Where to get the huge sum of money for the overtime pay when the leading departments kept the funds for this purpose under rigid control? How much money should be paid as bonuses to the workers who have worked so many extrashifts to accomplish so much? An enlarged meeting of the general Party branch at the plant agreed that a day's delay would cause losses of huge sums of money for both the plant and the refinery, and for the state as well, that it was the fundamental interests of the state and the actual conditions that should be given priority, that an enterprise in its attempt to fulfil its plan on schedule ought not to cling to the words of some regulations and provisions to the damage of the state property. And so the meeting decided to call the whole brigade into action to ensure the completion of the project on time and issue the overtime pay to all who worked extra hours. It was agreed that funds for the expenditures on the worksite be allocated at 13 percent of the estimated net profit so that the overtime pay and the bonus could be issued without a hitch. The brigade of 70 worked arduously for 100 days, completed the installation of the equipment five days ahead of time and put the refinery into operation with the first trial run, for which the fittings plant was given an award of 5,000 yuan. The net profit gained by the brigade's half-year work amounted to 220 thousand yuan. The higher authorities had promised the plant to issue an amount of bonuses equivalent to the sum of three months' pay of the plant's whole staff of 700, if it should realize a profit of 240 thousand yuan. The plant realized a profit of 420 thousand and issued a sum of bonuses for that year no greater than that fixed by plan. It was cited by the provincial department of finance for all that it had achieved.

(B) "Act on Your Own So Long as It Is Helpful to the State".
Management is needed for the effective realization of objectives. They can be realized in many ways, among which there must be the best choice. A manager should secure more ways of

doing things to choose from, particularly when the overall situation is at stake, and this would enable him to attain his goal best. To be good at making choices is a sign of the manager's ability to create and his dynamic role in business.

Assigning some tasks, the higher authorities may issue some directives or instructions concerning the ways or methods of doing things. If you consider your own way or method better than those prescribed by the higher authorities, you should explain it to them in time. If the matter tolerates no delay, you may act on your own and report at the same time or afterwards. Thus, the Yunnan provincial authorities decided to close down the county chemical fertilizer plants suffering losses for a long time and switch them to other productions. But the Longling County chemical fertilizer plant operated as before. The secret lay in the fact that the county, having many small hydroelectric power stations and being unable to hook them up with the regional grid at the time, had much electricity to spare, and if the fertilizer plant, the chief energy-consumer of the county, was closed down, that would mean a waste of power. The losses suffered by an operating fertilizer plant could be balanced by the profit gained by the power stations, and the county would be left with a surplus. Moreover, as chemical fertilizers were needed by the county's rural areas, local supply and transportation of them would be by far cheaper and more convenient than if they were purchased outside the county. And the existence of the fertilizer plant offered jobs and opportunities to the repair, transportation and supply and marketing organizations of the county which served it. These were the reasons why the Longling County did not obey the directive of the provincial authorities on this occasion.

The principle of refusing to obey the commands of the higher authorities on some occasions does not mean that a manager can do anything he wishes. Like the principle that an able general must not be hampered by the sovereign, it should be acted upon only under certain conditions.

And one of such conditions is: "if the situation offers the certainty of your victory". "Sun Zi", ch. 10, "Terrain", states, "If the situation offers the certainty of your victory, you must fight despite the sovereign's order not to fight. If the situation offers no prospect of winning victory, you must not fight despite the sovereign's order to fight." In a word, better succeed in violation of the orders from above than suffer defeat by keeping to them. The second of such conditions is: if it is "to serve the interests of his sovereign". (Ibid.) In our case, we must act in accordance with the interests of the state—representative of the best interests of our people who are the "sovereign" of the socialist enterprises.

Both these conditions for the disobedience of the commands of the higher authorities on some occasions must be given consideration to at the same time. For the stress on the first one alone could bring damage to the overall situation and the stress on the second one alone in the absence of the certainty of victory would probably lead to failure of an undertaking.

It is hard for one to disobey the commands from above on special occasions when it is necessary to do so, because the special measures for coping with the special occasions are hard to decide on. It is hard because under complex conditions risks are involve —the manager may commit mistakes in his decisions, take the blame for his presumption and bear the serious responsibility in case his decision should prove a failure. Consequently, only those leaders who have the courage to take risks on behalf of the interests of the state and excel at handling special problems with success can act upon the principle that "there are commands of the sovereign not to be obeyed" and are worthy to be called distinguished managers. The distinguished managers, far from being short-sighted and muddling along, consider themselves answerable not only to the higher authorities and focus their attention on something other than the "blame" they might some-day have to take. They are capable of grasping the meaning of the instructions of the higher authorities, determining the objec-tives of their own units in the light of the needs of the overall situation and working out specific guidelines and policies in line with the changing conditions. With a deep understanding of the uniformity of the interests of the state, the collective and the individual, they proceed from the interests of the state while studying the general line of the state, implementing policies and directing their subordinates. Their courage and resourcefulness come from their deep sense of responsibility and dedication to their work instead of their temperament and character; they base their decisions on the actual conditions and the knowledge of scientific dialectics, rather than sense perceptions and feelings. Such managers are rare and valuable, as Sun Wu wrote in Chapter 10, "Terrain", of his treatise: "... the general who thinks nothing of his fame when promoted, and shows courage in bearing his blames when demoted but whose only concern is to protect the people and to serve the interests of his sovereign, is the jewel of the state".

4. Speed Is Vital to War

Not once did Sun Wu discuss the thesis that speed is vital to war. "Sun Zi", ch. 11, "The Nine Varieties of Battleground", states, "Speed of action is the life of an army". Racing against time is of primary importance to military operations. Time is always one of the decisive factors contributing to the outcome of war. Marshal Liu Bocheng, celebrated Chinese strategist of our times, said, "When the five elements (referring to the task of operation, conditions of the enemy, conditions of ourselves, terrain and time) are not made clear, total collapse is to be expected".

Time and speed play a growing role in modern management. The current saying that efficiency is life and time is money represents a very important viewpoint. Speed, time and efficiency are related with each other, with time as the key link. Speed and efficiency find their expression in time. For a given task, the less the time spent on it, the higher the speed and the efficiency of work, and the more the time spent, the lower the speed and the efficiency.

Time seems to be something abundant, but it is rarer than anything else. Time is the most valuable thing of all, for it goes away, never to return. Time is the only "vehicle" in which decisions are made, management is conducted and jobs are done. Time is indispensable for doing anything. Famous Chinese poet Li Bai of the Tang Dynasty wrote, "Time passes by endless generations". A popular Chinese saying goes, "Time runs like a steed galloping past a crack". Almighty as you may be, you can never stop and draw back the running time.

When we say "Efficiency is life, and time is money", we mean something more than the ancient saying "Time is gold". Time is not only gold as such, it can multiply its value with better management and higher efficiency of work.

We should publicize the slogan that efficiency is life and time is money, to help better our management, create values with a higher efficiency, take the initiative into our hands with a greater speed of our advance and thus win victories in the competition for market.

(A) "Be the First in the Battlefield" and Take the Initiative into Your Hands.

"Sun Zi", ch. 6, "The Void and the Solid", states, "Generally, he who is the first in the battlefield and awaits his enemy enjoys ease; he who comes to the battlefield later and hurries into the battle knows weariness". The former finds himself in an active position, and the latter in a passive position. In order to come off victorious in competition, an enterprise engages itself in developing new technology and new products and often at one and the same time. Life has shown that the first one to succeed in the research work, put a new technology into production and meet the needs of the market with a new product is the "master" of that technology and that product. He who first puts onto the market a given product of a given quality at a given price takes the initiative in his hands and occupies the "commanding height" of the market. To wrest this "height" from him would take others much, much more painstaking efforts. In the words of Sun Wu, the first one to occupy a "commanding height" of the market is "awaiting the enemy" and "enjoys ease", while the others, "hurrying into the fight", "know weariness." Or in general military phraseology, this is a case when "you dominate the enemy, and are not dominated by him". In business, whoever wins the time wins the space, the initiative as well as the victory. Here, to be the first means "monopoly" of the market in a given period of time, which gives obvious superiority in time and space to the countries and regions with a patent system for new designs, new technology and new inventions.

To "be the first in the battlefield", to "arrive first as the swiftest", speed is needed. Sun Wu taught, "what is valued in war is the final victory, not protracted operations". (Chapter 2, "Waging War") He also explained his thesis, saying, "... what is required is quick victory. A long delay will cause the weapons blunted and the spirits of the troops dampened. A prolonged attack on a city will exhaust the army, and troops engaged in a protracted war will deplete the treasury of the state. When your weapons are blunted and your spirits dampened, when your strength exhausted and treasury emptied, other states will raise their troops against you, taking advantage of your straits. And no wise adviser will be able to remedy the situation". And he concluded, "Thus, what we have heard of is only simplicity in the quick decision of war, and we have never seen cleverness in prolonging it". Speed is essential, for speed is strength. With the direction of motion and other related conditions unchanged, the higher the speed, the greater the strength; and a strength at a high speed is irresistible. It is thanks to high speed the rushing water moves stones and birds of prey capture mice and hares. Speed can yield superiority: when one is stronger than the enemy, speed in attack leads to his victory; when one is weaker than the enemy, speed in retreat means his survival. In business management, speed plays a decisive role throughout the whole process of the activities of an enterprise. In the stage of making decisions, quick acquisition of accurate information is valued more than anything else, and a timely choice and a snap decision made are the key to success. In the stage of production management, speed is essential to the effective investment of capital, the preparation of a new product for mass production and its output. Speed means shorter production cycles, lower production costs and greater competitive power. In the stage of marketing and competition for market, it is imperative to get the products onto the market at once, for quick sales means quick circulation of the funds of the enterprise, which contributes to its healthy development much as unblocked blood circulation does to the metabolism of a healthy organism. So speed signifies the vitality of an enterprise; and generally, an enterprise managed effectively is one working at a high speed. In June 1982, the zinc-plated iron wire plant in the city of Xiangfan, Hubei Province, learned from the newspapers "Economic Information" and "Market" that the supply of a certain kind of wire rod was beginning to fall short of demand and decided immediately to increase the output of that product and enlarge its stock. In October, the commercial authorities, as was expected, contacted the plant for business negotiations and undertook to sell all the 400 tons of the wire produced. The speed with which production was arranged on getting a piece of accurate information brought the small plant an entra profit of 12 thousand yuan that year. The June 1 shoe factory in Beijing produced over 30 samples of its products for a foreign merchant the very next day after the business negotiation and concluded right away a transaction worth 600 thousand U.S. dollars with the customer who appreciated the speed very much. In the first quarter of 1983, Hong Kong exported as much as over 186 million Hong Kong dollars' worth of wired telephone sets, an increase of nearly 19 times over the same period of the previous year. Speed in response was the chief contributor to the huge gains. Originally the U.S. Government stipulated that telephone sets could only be let by the American Telephone and Telegraph Company (AT&T), and their purchase by any individual was illegal. In 1982, it cancelled the patent right of the AT&T and permitted any person to buy telephone sets freely. Such being the case, the 80 million American families and all the public and private institutions of the United States became the potential buyers of telephone sets. The Hong Kong manufacturers, on getting wind of the sudden boom of the US telephone market, switched the radio and digital watch production to the production of telephone sets and "swooped down upon" the U.S. telephone market. And the success was astounding.

(B) Be Quick, But with Precise Timing; Seize the Right Moment.

"Sun Zi", ch. 5, "Momentum", states, "when the torrent of water rolls boulders along, it is because of its momentum. When a hawk swooping down crushes the body of its prey, it is because of its well-regulated strike. So, a good warrior's momentum is overpowering and his well-timed strike brief and forceful. He has the potential of a fully drawn crossbow and times his strike as when he releases the trigger". With an overpowering momentum, the troops in action are irresistible, just like a momentary strike of a hawk crushes a bird and a sudden leap of a tiger succumbs an animal. Speed and timing are the two factors of the strike of a hawk and the leap of a tiger. Here, we are going to discuss the role of timing.

Timing involves rhythm and the right moment. When a hawk is going to catch its prey, it hovers for some time trying to make its swoop from a right distance; when a tiger is going to bear down on a deer, it first crouches in wait and then leaps forward to attack. They observe, judge, plan, gather their energy and try to seize the right moment for action. Business managers ought to know the role of timing as well as speed and be good at grasping the right rhythm and the right moment. They ought to avoid using their skills in vain, at a wrong moment, and "alternate tension with relaxation" at an opportune moment. When there is no compromise between speed and timing, the former ought to give way to the latter, because one cannot be born when the time is not yet ripe, and things cannot be done when conditions are not yet available.

In 1979, on the eve of the traditional "Mid-Autumn Festival", the confectioneries in Fujian and Guangdong provinces produced a batch of "moon cakes" for the Hong Kong market. The cakes sold briskly, at the price of the equivalent of RMB 1 yuan apiece. The confectioneries, encouraged, made more cakes, only to leave the second batch with no buyers in Hong Kong even at ten cents apiece. This was because the Festival was then over. The price of the "moon cakes" varied with the elapse of time, and the right time for their brisk sales was the one week preceding the Festival—no earlier, no later. Managers of the confectioneries remembered "speed" in business, but forgot "timing", and so they asked for trouble.

To be quick with precise timing is the key to good business. The 1978 World Cup Football Tournament with the West German and the Dutch teams vying for championship and the 1982 one with the Italian and the French teams contending for supremacy created quite a stir in Europe, and goods printed with designs of footballs and prize cups soared in price. The year 1981 saw the wedding of Prince Charles of Great Britain, and the confectionery owners lost no time in printing the photograph of the prince and his wife on the packages of their products which sold very well even at a price 20-30 percent higher than that of those without the photograph. Of course, time was essential to such sales; the surplus goods had to be sold at a reduced price when the time was over.

5. "There Can Never Be Too Much Deception in War"

"Sun Zi", ch. 1, "Reckoning", states, "All warfare is done by trickery". Cao Cao's commentary on this statement was: "There is nothing constant in warfare but the way of deception". Li Quan's was: "An army can never overemphasize deception". Mei Chengyao's was: "Without deception there is no manoeuvre; without manoeuvre there cannot be victory over the enemy". And Zhang Yu commented, "Though a war is resorted to for the sake of humanity and righteousness, the way to victory is bound to be through deception". Deception is a tactical means for the end of winning victory and has been resorted to in warfare as a matter of course since ancient times.

Deception is a tactical means for contention. It is common in the life-and-death struggle between capitalist enterprises and has been developed to a "new height" of "modernization" under the guise of "co-prosperity" so as to make their scramble even more covert. In recent years when China began to carry out a policy of opening to the outside world, some lawbreaking foreign merchants went all out to cheat the Chinese with their tricks.

What an approach, then, should we, business managers of socialist China, have toward deception as a means of warfare? So long as there is warfare, competition and contention, there will be people resorting to deception. With deception, just as with the employment of spies, we should, generally speaking, know how to rise above it, but we should not remain ignorant of it, or else we would get the worst of it. Handling our foreign trade, we have to deal with a lot of foreign capitalists, which is a kind of struggle in itself. We have to know the tactics needed for the struggle, know the opponents and ourselves and be able to see through their tricks. The foreign capitalists will always try to cheat money out of us by every possible means including deception. Even inside China, while most of our enterprises uphold justice and socialist morality, there are some people who stop at nothing to gain profit for themselves. Some upstarts who profited by deception were brought to light in recent years in the campaigns against the criminal activities in the economic field.

In Japan, the gourmet powder had once been dull of sale. Then it found a good market after the one-millimetre-across holes in the lid of a bottle containing it had been replaced by the ones one and a half millimetre across which let out a little too much of the powder each time the consumer remaining in the dark used it. The Japanese bosses of gourmet powder production were practising deception, playing on people's faith in what they have been used to. As a socialist country, China, of course, will never resort to such a trickery of sales promotion. But we have to learn to see through such deception and follow the advice of our forebears: "Never harbour malice against others, and never forget to defend yourself, either."

Three kinds of ways of deception are listed in Chapter 1, "Reckoning", of the ancient military treatise "Sun Zi":

1. To conceal the truth so that the enemy can be taken by surprise. Sun Wu wrote: "... when capable of attack, you must seem incapable; when ready to attack, you must seem unready. When your target is near, give the impression that it is far away; when your target is far wawy, give the impression that it is near." "Anger the enemy general, that he may become irritable. Pretend to be inferior, that he may grow arrogant".

2. To defeat the enemy by luring him with minor gains. Sun Wu wrote: "Offer the enemy a bait to lure him; manoeuvre the enemy into confusion and crush him". "When the enemy troops rest easy, rob them of their rest. When the enemy forces are united, disunite them".

3. To avoid disadvantages and strike the enemy's weakness. Sun Wu wrote: "When he has secured his position, prepare against him; where he has superior strength, avoid encounters with him". Attack where the enemy is unprepared; act when he does not suspect it".

During the ten years of tumult (1966-1976) in China, merchants from a certain country went into the site of the Commodities Fair at Guangzhou with a "Little Red Book" held high to show their "sincerity" in extolling the "great achievement" of China's campaign for "learning from Dazhai". This was done with the purpose of gaining a whole lot of "preferential prices" from some Chinese negotiators who would consider them as "friendly traders". This was deception—"Pretend to be inferior that he may grow arrogant", so as to "get him unawares".

In many enterprises and trading companies abroad there is a "public relations department"whose job is to entertain guests, make gifts and seek favourable connections. According to the press, the Japanese enterprises spent in 1981 a record total of 3,300 billion yen (an equivalent of about 13.5 billion U.S. dollars), or an average of 9 billion yen (or 3,700 U.S. dollars) per day, on giving their clients dinners, entertaining them with golf games and sending them gifts. In 1981, the U.S. enterprises were reported to have spent over 9 billion U.S. dollars on gifts including cars, motorcycles, TV sets, refrigerators, microwave ovens, sets of furniture and minor objects such as digital watches, fountain pens, ball-point pens, handkerchiefs, scarves, etc., some of which were goods in great demand and even those bought from other countries.

The reform of China's foreign trade system in the recent years, generally speaking, has been going on smoothly, but there has evolved a tendency of decentralism and departmental selfishness. There were instances of the Chinese trading organizations competing with each other and let each other down in their dealings with the foreign traders. Quite a few of foreign and Hong Kong merchants, taking advantage of the confusion among the Chinese themselves, made fortunes for themselves, to the damage of the interests of China both economically and politically. Now China conducts her foreign trade in line with a unitary policy, with unified planning and unified arrangements, which will benefit the country and prevent her from getting duped.

To counteract deception, we can and should use some techniques and tactical means of deception in our dealings with the merchants from the capitalist countries. Thus, in business negotiations falsehood is often shown to protect ourselves and keep the other party unprepared. Before a negotiation, both parties will always keep their own intentions in secret, for whoever knows the "cards" in his partner's hands have the initiative in the negotiation. This is why the negotiators show what is false and conceal what is true more often than not. And we can naturally do so "on just grounds", "to our advantage" and "with restraint" in the framework of socialist ethics. The principle of avoiding disadvantages and striking the opponent's weakness can also be followed in the contention on market and in business management in general.

So far we have had a sketchy description of the three main stages of business management—decision-making, production management and competition for market—in the light of some of the scientific ideas and methods expounded in the ancient treatise "Sun Wu's Art of War" and the actual conditions of modern business. The three stages of management activities are related to each other. They form a system, a process of endless development in spirals, whose management is a kind of systems control, as can be seen from the following chart:

Chart 2

Flow Process Chart of Business Management

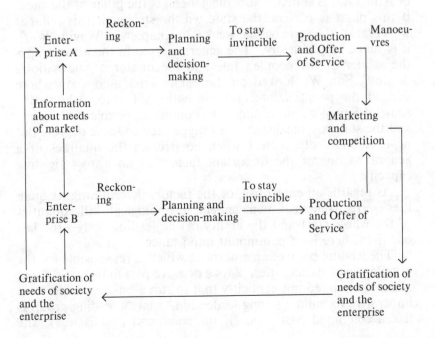

Chapter IV
"Five Virtues" Required of a Commander
—Essentials for a Business Leader

The military treatise "Sun Zi" discusses time and again the position, role and essential qualities of the commander. In its Chapter 1, "Reckoning", command is listed as one of the five key factors determining the outcome of a war and the question of "which of the two commanders has greater ability" as one of the seven comparisons to be made of the two warring sides, second only to the question of "which of the two sovereigns is the representative of 'the Right Way' ". In Chapter 3, "The Strategy of Attack", it is stated, "Now the general is the pillar of the state: if this pillar is perfect, the state will be strong; if this pillar is with cracks, the state will be weak." In Chapter 2, "Waging War", it is stated emphatically, "The general versed in the art of war is the arbiter of the people's fate and the master of the nation's destiny". Sun Wu looked on the commander as one on whom depend the people's fate and the nation's future. Admittedly, some of Sun Wu's views about the commander's role in the army and the state are idealistic; it is exaggerated to some degree. But he is undoubtedly correct when he stresses the qualities of a general as one of the important factors of an army's fighting capacity.

As regards an enterprise, of the factors determining its qualities—effectiveness of management, technological skills, qualities of the whole staff and the ability of the leading body—the last one listed here is of paramount importance.

The leading body of an enterprise which is responsible for the orientation of its activities, plays a decisive part in its work. Deng Xiaoping pointed out explicitly that to run a business well, "it is imperative to build a strong leadership," that "a leading group is like a command post" and "if the command post is weak, the operations cannot be effective". (Selected Works of Deng Xiaoping, Eng. ed., FLP, Beijing, 1984, p. 18-19)

The factory director is at the head of the leading body of an enterprise. Deng Xiaoping wrote, "The main thing is to select good persons for the two top posts in each enterprise. If these two dare to act, they can carry the whole staff along with them." (Ibid., p. 40). In an enterprise, the director occupies a decisive position because authority is called for in the modern large-scale production where a unified arrangement and coordinated organization of work is essential to all working procedures, all links and departments of the enterprise. This is just like fighting a war where lack of a unified disposition and an authoritative military command would be simply inconceivable, as thousands of troops have to attack, retreat, defend, outflank the enemy or penetrate the enemy forces. As the director or manager has the management of an enterprise in his hands and leads the whole staff in conducting its productive activities in accordance with a set policy for the attainment of a set goal, his competence is the key to the success of the enterprise, and his qualities are the thing on which hinges its fate. And the Secretary of the Party Committee plays an important part in ensuring the implementation of the policies in the enterprise, the achievement of its objectives and its steady growth by exercising ideological and political leadership. In organizing a good leading body of an enterprise with its members more revolutionary-minded, younger in average age, better enducated and professionally more competent, the main thing is to select the right person for the post of director or manager.

"Sun Zi", ch. 1, "Reckoning", states, "By command are meant the general's qualities of wisdom, good faith, humanity, courage and strictness." Zhang Yu's commentary on this statement reads, "Only with all these five virtues available can one be made commander". This is also true of the "commander" of an enterprise.

1. "The Right Way"—Soul of a Commander

Chapter 1, "Reckoning", of "Sun Zi" puts forward the fundamental problem for war, the problem of appraising war in terms of the five key factors and making seven comparisons, and, in order of priority, it places "the Right Way" ahead of "Command" in its discussions. Statements about "the Right Way" and "Command" throughout the treatise lead us to the realization that, firstly, as decisive factors of the outcome of a war, "the Right Way" comes first, and "Command" second; secondly, as regards the relation between "the Right Way" and "Command", the former directs the latter, and the latter submits itself to the former, which means the political line determines the personnel policy; and thirdly, good political qualities are to be the first thing to be required of a candidate for the post of a commander, and the political maturity of a commander should be placed on the top of the list of his qualities.

What is meant by "the Right Way"? It implies politics, political line and guidelines. War is the continuation of politics and serves the will of the ruling class. Everything—command, laws, institutions, virtues, and so on—must be subordinated to the political line of the ruling class, and there can never be virtues sitting above politics. In his commentary on "Sun Zi", Jia Lin wrote, "With 'the Right Way' as his soul, a commander who wins the soldiers' hearts by sharing weal and woe with them shares, as a matter of course, the mind of his sovereign". "The Right Way" referred to here is "the mind" of the sovereign, or politics which directs the military commander and determines the "five virtues". "The Right Way" is the thing by which a commander's virtues, or qualities, of "wisdom, good faith, humanity, courage and strictness" are judged. For a business manager of socialist China, to make "the Right Way" his soul ought to mean that he should always improve his moral qualities, and his political integrity in particular, uphold the "Four Cardinal Principles", work conscientiously under the guidance of the guidelines and policies of the state, defend the interests of the state and the people and strive to make his business a success with a dedication of a pioneer so that more and more products are turned out to satisfy the needs of social development and those of the growth of the enterprise itself.

Reform should be looked on as an integral part of "the Right Way" of socialist entrepreneur. Reform will be carried on throughout the drive for the socialist modernization of the country, reform of the aspects of the relations of production that are no longer suited to the development of the forces of production and those of the superstructure that are no longer suited to the economic base, aiming at perfecting our socialist system and bringing its superiority into full play.

Sun Wu was a "reformist" of his time. A representative of the emerging landlord class, he pointed out, "War is a matter of primary importance to the State.... Hence a thorough study of it is not to be dispensed with". (Chapter 1, "Reckoning") This was by far a more positive approach than the ambiguous attitude of Confucious on the question of war. Sun Wu gave a materialist interpretation of the concept of "Heaven". He wrote, "By heavenly timeliness are meant day and night, overcast and fine, winter's cold and summer's heat and other factors of weathers and seasons affecting war". (Chapter 1, "Reckoning") He was against forecasting the outcome of a war by superstitious means. He wrote, "This foreknowledge cannot be elicited from spirits and gods, nor can it be inferred from the analogy with anything experienced in the past, nor can it be tested and verified by the measurements of the movements of the celestial bodies. It can be obtained only from men who know the enemy situation". (Chapter 13, "Espionage") For the age of superstition when "Heaven" was revered as god, this statement of Sun Wu's was clearly progressive in character. His statement, "... those who were renowned to be good at employing troops moved when it was advantageous to do so; and halted when it was not". (Chapter 11, "The Nine Varieties of Battleground"), seemed heretical to the Confucians who asserted, "What the superior men value is righteousness; what the small people value is advantage".

Any reform will be thwarted by the outdated ideas and resisted by the forces of convention. But without reform there will be no progress—for a society, and an enterprise as well. Without a drive for reform, no manager could possibly bring a new look into his enterprise. Luo Xingang, the hero in the film "Blood Is Always Hot", dedicated to the cause of reform, was ready to "lubricate the rust-ridden gear wheels of economy" with his blood and get them back to motion. Real advocates of reform in China today, such as Bu Xinsheng, Wang Zepu, Qin Shiming and Xia Dinghu, have made a success of their efforts to bring their enterprises progress only as a result of their resolute resistance to pressures from all sides.

A comnander should be qualified by his political integrity. Sun Wu wrote, "The general who thinks nothing of his fame when promoted and shows courage in bearing his blames when demoted, but whose only concern is to protect the people and to serve the interests of his sovereign is the jewel of the state".

This statement about what is a good general offers much for us to think over and learn from. In socialist China, a good business manager takes Marxist theory as his guide and the "Four Cardinal Principles" as his code of conduct. He always puts the interests of the state and the people above anything else, never seeking personal fame and never shifting his responsibility. He is "the first to worry about the cares of the country and the last to share the happiness of the whole nation". He is set on carrying out a reform and takes pains to find the way to get his enterprise onto a new height. All this is the expression of "the Right Way" for the leader of a socialist enterprise.

For many years An Zhengdong, now Deputy Governor of Heilongjiang Province, suffered injustices and knew frustrations in all their bitterness, but he kept his faith in the Communist Party and the cause of socialism. And Chen Xiuyun, Party secretary at the factory where An Zhengdong worked when wronged and framed up, volunteered to give him protection and promotion. Their story shows that the leading cadres who are loyal to the cause of revolution are really "jewels" of our nation, that "the Right Way" they follow is incomparably superior to that expounded by Sun Wu.

2. None of the Essential Qualities to Be Neglected

"Sun Zi", ch. 1, "Reckoning", states, "By command are meant the general's qualities of wisdom, good faith, humanity, courage and strictness". Wang Xi gave his commentary on this statement as follows: "Wisdom presupposes foresight, sober-mindedness, capability for deliberation and knowledge of tactics. Good faith means uniformity in executing orders. Humanity implies kindness, compassion and popularity. Courage signifies fearlessness and resolution in upholding righteousness. Strictness is understood as prestige with which to awe and unite the minds of the subordinates. The five things supplement each other, and none of them can be dispensed with. Cao Cao said, 'It is a must for a general to possess all the five virtues.' " In our view, Sun Wu's thesis about the "five virtues" required of a general and Wang Xi's commentary on it can give us much food for thought when we discuss the question of what essential qualities are to be required of our business managers today.

(1) Wisdom. The ancients said, "Sun Wu emphasized the role of wisdom". That Sun Wu listed wisdom as the first of the "five virtues" testifies to the great attention he paid to the ability of a leader to command. Time and again he expounded in his treatise the significance of the wisdom of a commander. He wrote, "The general versed in the art of war is the arbiter of the people's fate and the master of the nation's destiny". (Chapter 2, "Waging War"); "The ability to estimate the enemy situation correctly, to keep the initiative in his own hands while fighting for victory, to find out the accessibility of the terrain and to calculate distances is what is required of a great commander. He who knows these things and fights with his knowledge is sure to win; he who fights without knowing these things is sure to be defeated". (Chapter 10, "Terrain"); "A general has to know all about these five key factors". (i.e. "the Right Way," "heavenly timeliness", "terrain", "command" and "institutions") (Chapter 1, "Reckoning"); "A wise commander will always blend his considerations of the favourable conditions with those of the unfavourable ones. Keeping in view the favourable conditions, he will be able to fulfil his plans; keeping in view the unfavourable conditions, he will be able to remove his trouble." (Chapter 8, "Endless Tactical Adaptations"); "The commander who thoroughly understand the advantages of the endless tactical adaptations knows the art of using troops. The commander who does not know the advantages of the endless tactical adaptations may know the ground but he cannot make the best of it. The commander who does not understand the art of tactical adaptations may know the 'five

advantages', but he cannot make the best use of his troops." These statements of Sun Wu's point to the need for a commander to know strategy, pros and cons, flexibility in waging war, and so on.

Wang Chong (27-c. 97 A.D.), noted philosopher of the Han Dynasty, said, "Wisdom is strength". And Francis Bacon also said, "Knowledge itself is power." A business leader should, like the military commanders, be equipped with knowledge including that referred to by Sun Wu, a wide range of knowledge of production and business operation.

Our age is one of vigorous advance of science and technology, one of knowledge explosion, one of information explosion. Business management is a frontier science involving the knowledge of both natural and social sciences. So a business manager today cannot be wise and resourceful unless he arms himself with extensive knowledge.

Our age is one of fierce economic contention and competition, both international and domestic, which is in essence a battle for talents and a battle of wits. Sun Wu wrote in Chapter 3, "The Strategy of Attack," of his treatise, "The wisest policy of a general is to frustrate the enemy's strategy". This can also be the case with modern business management. Sun Wu was the first to set forth the idea of what is called "contingency views" in modern management theory. He wrote, "When my advices are taken after the advantageous and disadvantageous circumstances are made clear, effort should be made to create favourable situations which will be a contributor to the victory of war. By 'creating favourable situations' I mean that one should always take actions as are dictated by what is advantageous". Here Sun Wu advocated creating favourable situations on the basis of weighing advantages and disadvantages carefully and winning victory by adapting oneself with all flexibility to the changing circumstances. This can never be done without sufficient knowledge.

The historical novel "The Romance of Three Kingdoms" describes Zhuge Liang as a supernatural personage when he is portrayed as being capable of conjuring up the east wind to help his attack by fire. This is, of course, untrue, but Prime Minister Zhuge Liang had indeed a wide range of knowledge, including that of astronomy and geography. The old Chinese saying that

"Three cobblers are worth a Zhuge Liang" is a tribute to his wisdom. Military commanders and business managers alike should arm themselves with as much knowledge as possible.

History knows many successful Chinese and foreign entrepreneurs who were learned people. The story of the Kunming machine tools plant manufacturing the much-needed shoe-trees-making milling machines offers an axample of the importance of the expert professionals to an enterprise.

V. I. Lenin said long ago: "Management necessarily implies competency,... a knowledge of all the conditions of production down to the last detail and of the latest technology of your branch of production is required; you must have had a certain scientific training". (V. I. Lenin, Selected Works, Eng. ed., Moscow, 1965, Vol. 30, p. 428) Our business managers should train themselves as experts who know a lot about science and technology and are at the same time well versed in management.

Modern management often takes the form of collective control. Therefore, a rational intellectual structure of a leading body is essential. A leading body should be composed of an army of experts in various fields of work such as those who are good at making decisions, those who know how to organize production and many, many others, so that they complement each other intellectually and double and triple and quadruple the intellectual capacity of the leading body as a whole.

We do not mean, of course, to say that a business manager should learn everything indiscriminately. A business manager should first and foremost master the knowledge needed by his own duty right now. It would be desirable that he applies himself to the study of various subjects in addition.

A business manager should make special effort to develop his ability to act, ability to make decisions, ability to organize the personnel, ability to coordinate and communicate, ability to judge and create and ability to respond to changes correctly —proof of his worth as a competent business leader of the day. He should develop these abilities, on the one hand, by mastering a rich store of knowledge and, on the other, by learning hard from his day-to-day work experience which gives him knowledge of life.

(2) Good faith. In his commentary on "Sun Zi", Du Mu wrote, "Good faith calls for getting rid of people's puzzlement about penalties and rewards." Wang Xi's commentary reads, "Good faith means uniformity in executing orders." It is our understanding that "good faith" presupposes trustworthiness in giving awards and meting out penalties.

A business manager should keep his word faithfully to win people's trust. He must be as good as his word, acting resolutely according to what he says, and free from any empty talk. He must be strict and fair in meting out rewards and punishments. He must win the trust of his whole staff with the credit he has with them and gain the appreciation of the public with his good reputation and record.

History knows a lot of instances of winning trust and prestige by means of good faith. Upon entering the employment of Duke Hsiao (reign 361-338 B.C.) of the state of Chin, Shang Yang asked to introduce reforms. When it was approved by the Duke and the reforms were ready to be promulgated, in order to win the people's trust, he had a wooden pillar thirty feet high set up at the south gate of the market and offered a reward of ten gold pieces to anyone who would move it to the north gate. The people were sceptical and no one dared move it. Then a reward of fifty gold pieces was offered. A man moved the pillar and received the reward, proving that the authorities meant what they said. Steps taken by Shang Yang to win the people's faith in him helped to win their faith in his reforms and thus create favourable conditions for carrying them out. To stop theft of public property, the Fuzhou pencil factory made the stipulation that any stealer of public property be expelled from the factory or be placed on probation in the factory and demoted on the wage scale. And it did stop such thefts with just one case dealt with in strict compliance with the stipulation. The factory also got rid of smoking within the area of its workshops by enforcing only once its stipulation that anyone who smoked once within that area be fined 48 yuan.

To win the trust of others, one must be honest and sincere with them. Honesty is a quality indispensable to a leader. Honesty is needed in dealing with anyone inside or outside your organization, from the higher authorities or among your subordinates.

Nothing can more easily infringe on the prestige of a manager than his being found cheating. To our regret, there are some business leaders who are apt to offer their subordinates promises and fail to make them good, give the higher authorities exaggerated accounts of their achievements, reward and punish with no sense of inpartiality and tear up contracts with other organizations at will. Apparently, such leaders can only make a mess of business management.

Creditability is strength for a business manager, and his honesty can be an advantage of his enterprise. If he is determined to win the trust of the customers with the high quality of his products, the enterprise will not allow its defective products to appear on the market; if the enterprise guarantees to repair, replace or take back those of its products that do not live up to standards, the workers will do their best to improve the quality of their products and come out on top in competition with their high quality.

Like the products, credit, trust and reputation are things of value. It is "good faith" and "trustworthiness" that have brought prosperity to the old enterprises with their famous products, such as the Zhang Xiaoquan scissors store in Hangzhou, the Goubuli steamed stuffed buns store in Tianjin and the Maotai winery in Guizhou. Managers who do not understand this can mar the reputation of their famous-brand products. And those who should cheat the consumers with scamp work and stint material or inferior imitations in their frenzied pursuit of profit can only ruin their enterprises.

Of course, trustworthiness does not mean sticking to something out of date without any change, for that would be stupidity rather than good faith.

(3) Humanity. In his commentary on "Sun Zi", Wang Xi wrote, "Humanity implies kindness, compassion and popularity". Du Mu commented, "Without humanity, a general will not share the hardships of starvation and toil with the troops". And He Shi commented, "Without humanity, one cannot unite the multitude and show kindness to the rank-and-file". Stressing humanity, Sun Wu wrote in Chapter 10, "Terrain", of his treatise that when a general "regards his men as infants" or "as his beloved sons", they will take any risk and fight to the death. This is quite true in war.

General Yue Fei (1103-1142 A.D.) was well known for his kind treatment of his soldiers and the invincibility of his army whose officers and men were united as one.

A socialist business manager imbued with the spirit of humanity treats his subordinates as his class brothers and sisters, practising democracy in production and management. He conducts political enducation among them and concerns himself with their well-being. He enlightens them with reason and moves them with feelings, showing good sense. Only in this way can he achieve unity of minds and rally the whole staff around the leadership in their concerted efforts to make their enterprise full of vigor and vitality and push it forward along a path of its own toward the set objectives. In a factory of Harbin, the canteen was once in a bad way, as those who went to mess early could have anything they wished while those who went on time could have what was left and those who went late from their job could have nothing they wished. This cut into the morale of the workers and the staff members and affected the production. The managers studied the problem and soon found a solution to it to the satisfaction of all. They proved "close friends" to the workers.

Under socialism, the ethical concept of "humanity" can be extended to one dealing with the relations between an enterprise and the consumers and those among enterprises. Thus, "humanity" is felt when an enterprise meets the needs of the customers with its high-quality products and service, when it does everything with the customers in mind and refuses to benefit itself at the cost of others. "Humanity" is also felt in competition with other enterprises. For instance, a plant of war production in Northeast China refrained from undertaking the production of the much sought-after goods for civilian use when it was faced with the problem of switching to some new products, though it had superiority in conditions of production and technical personnel over the civilian enterprises. It made good use of its superior conditions to produce what was beyond their power to "make good omissions and deficiencies" instead of trying to knock them out. This is a competition with consideration for others and without scramble for profit, the diametrical opposite to the life-and-death contention among the self-seeking capitalist enterprises.

(4) Courage. Different commentators gave different interpretations to "courage" in the terminology of "Sun Zi". For instance, Du Mu wrote, "Courage is the will to wrest victory without the least hesitation, making full use of the situation". Wang Xi wrote, "Courage signifies fearlessness and resolution in upholding righteousness". And He Shi wrote, "Without courage, making decisions and waging war would be impossible". They were right in writing these commentaries. Here we would like to emphasize that courage should be backed by resourcefulness. In "Sun Zi with Annotations by Eleven Scholars", Du Mu quoted Wu Qi (?-381 B.C.), another strategist of the Warring States Period, as saying, "Generally, people judge of a general by his courage. But courage is but one of the qualities a general should possess. One who has courage alone must not be made general, for he would be rash to engage the enemy without considering whether it is advantageous." That is to say, the courage of taking rash actions in ignorance of where the basic interests lie is no quality of a general. A commander must have both courage and resourcefulness, for courage divorced from resourcefulness is but recklessness and resourcefulness separated from courage is pedantry. The "empty-city stratagem" of Zhuge Liang was the fruit of both courage and resourcefulness. Sima Yi, frightened by his enemy's "empty city", missed the opportunity of taking Zhuge Liang prisoner. His hesitation and lack of courage showed his intellectual inferiority to Zhuge Liang.

Courage is called for in business decision-making. It happens that time can wait no more for a decision when things have not yet been made clear, and the manager may take a risk or miss an opportunity. This is when the manager's courage and ability are challenged.

Courage should be fostered and promoted in the drive for socialist modernization of the country. He who has the courage to carry on reforms and create new things never rests content with things as they are and never rests on his laurels. He would rather take risks in pioneering new undertakings than sit with folded hands, keeping away from any trouble. He dares make decisions and acts so long as what he does is in the interests of the state and within the limits permitted by the policy of the government. What our cause needs is contingents of the pioneering-type business leaders with remarkable wisdom and courage.

Courage can have its meaning only with certain conditions present. Subjectively, they are moral qualities meaning utter dedication, sense of responsibility and dauntlessness in fighting for justice; resourcefulness meaning great intellectual capacity; and drive meaning boldness and resolution in making decisions. Objectively, these conditions are the acquisition and study of information from inside and outside the enterprise, a must for a decision-maker who wants to know well how things stand with his business.

Courage in business management used to be misunderstood as that shown in "charging at the head of the rank-and-file". People used to say that a leader should be as much sweaty as the workers are greasy. The idea may be a boon in certain circumstances, but it would be unadvisable for a business manager to devote his time and energy mainly to the productive labour and daily routine as an average worker, for that would be a case of "seizing a grain of sesame and giving up a watermelon", as a popular Chinese saying goes.

(5) Strictness. In his commentary on "Sun Zi", Du Mu wrote, "Strictness means prestige and penalties with which to put the troops in order". Wang Xi wrote, "Strictness is understood as prestige with which to awe and unite the minds of the subordinates". And He Shi wrote, "Without strictness you cannot subdue the tough and unite the many". These are quite sensible statements. Strictness suggests seriousness and impartiality in enforcing military discipline and executing laws and orders.

Strictness can never be too important for war, for the army has to exert itself as a collective united in will and action, and a motley crowd in sheer disorder would be no army at all. This is why outstanding generals throughout the ages have insisted on getting their troops highly disciplined.

In the later years of the Spring and Autumn Period in Chinese history, Duke Jing of the state of Chi appointed Tian Rangju commander of his troops which were to fight off the allied forces of the states of Jin and Yan. He also appointed his favourite official named Zhuang Jia military supervisor. The two agreed to meet at the gateway of the camp at noonday the next day. Tian arrived there ahead of time, but Zhuang came tipsy only toward evening and put the blame for his being late on the farewell dinner given him by his relatives. Tian Rangju denounced him angrily as one ready to cling to the comfort of his family in disregard of the interests of the state. Then he called the military disciplinarian to him and asked, "How to deal with one who is late without any reason according to military law?" "Behead him!" was the reply. Scared out of his wits, Zhuang Jia sent an urgent message to the sovereign, asking for help. But Tian Rangju had already had him beheaded for all to see before the messenger was back at the camp. When the messenger hurried in and showed the Duke's instruction to pardon Zhuang Jia, Tian said, "There are commands of the sovereign which need not be obeyed by a general in military action". And he asked the military disciplinarian, "What to do with one who gallops about the military camp?" "Behead him!" was the reply. Tian said, "But it won't do to kill an envoy of the sovereign". Then he ordered that the envoy's follower and a horse pulling his chariot be killed and the convoy himself be sent back to the Duke, and he set out at once with his troops. The morale of the troops was greatly raised, and no one disobeyed orders and violated discipline. The enemy troops withdrew without fighting a battle and Tian Rangju chased them until all the lost territory was recovered.

Strictness is what guarantees the serious enforcement of military discipline and the combat-worthiness of the troops. This is also true to business management. In the Fujian electronic equipment plant, many people used to come late for work and leave early; they would come and go as they pleased during work hours. As a result, productivity of the plant was low. The switch of the plant to a joint venture with the investments of a foreign corporation introduced the practice of giving handsome rewards and imposing heavy punishments. Now everyone is busy at work during work hours except for the ten-minute breaks in the morning and in the afternoon. In the past two years, the plant raised its annual average output value per person by 570 percent and its total output value by 670 percent. Giving "handsome rewards", the plant stressed the promotion of the workers' well-being on the basis of the growth of production instead of handing out bonuses indiscreetly. Imposing "heavy punishments", the plant stressed the rigorous enforcement of the rules and regulations to foster and maintain a fine style of work. Thus, in addition to checking on work attendance with automatic machines for sign-in, the Corporation stipulated that the penalty for anyone who came for once one minute late for work was to withhold the bonus due to him that month and the 20-yuan "floating wage" for the month. With a view to keep environmental sanitation, the administration declared that anyone who spit on the ground for once would be denied the bonus due to him for half a year and the "floating wage" for that period totalling 120 yuan. The first one to come late for work after the promulgation of the stipulations turned out to be a deputy manager of the Chinese side. The chief manager, his compatriot, called him in and pointed out his mistake. The deputy manager admitted his fault and was punished as was stipulated. The leaders of the plant agreed that with lax enforcement of the regulations the long-standing bad habits of some workers could never be overcome, and the regulations would remain on paper, but with the regulations enforced as they should be, the workers would observe them in all seriousness. Up to now, there has been only one case of fining one person spitting on the ground, and very few came late for work or left early from their jobs in the last two years or more.

There must be reason and propriety about enforcing discipline. Tolerance and strictness must be shown just right, for excessive gentleness spells laxity and excessive rigidity breakage. Strictness in enforcing laws and orders must be accompanied by good faith; unpredictable changes in policy and a "just-this-once" approach should be avoided. Strictness without good faith is bound to ruin the inviolability of discipline and the militancy of the contingent. And strictness must go hand in hand with impartiality. All men must be equal before law, and those responsible for the enforcement of law must be upright and invulnerable to personal considerations. The above-mentioned instance of the denial of bonus to the deputy manager made a great impact on the workers of his plant. This was a case where good faith and impartiality in strict enforcement of the regulations asserted themselves.

A commander, by and large, should possess all the above-mentioned "five virtues" of wisdom, good faith, humanity, courage and strictness without neglecting any one of them. But, since nothing is perfectly pure and nobody absolutely perfect in this world, we do not mean to say that a commander should be best qualified by these "five virtues" for his post. He may behave well with respect to one of them and not so well with respect to another.

A modern enterprise is managed by a leading body of a number of people who differ in their qualification with respect to these "five virtues". Only a leading body made up of people better qualified by some of the "five virtues" and those better qualified by others can practise collective leadership in a concerted, fruitful effort.

Life has shown that the personnel structure of the leading body of people possessing all the "five virtues" and each behaving best with respect to one or another of them is more rational and more powerful than that of the leading body of people all distinguishing themselves only in one respect. The reason why Liu Bang (256-195 B.C.) was the first to capture Xianyang, capital of the Chin Dynasty, and founded his own dynasty of Han was that he had under his command a group of officials and generals each excelling at one thing or another, such as Xiao He who was charged with financial affairs and administration, Han Xin who was in command of his troops in action and Zhang Liang who offered him strategic plans and advices, and Liu Bang himself knew the art of organizing his "leading body" of able men with their respective fine qualities and getting them work in concert. In the Period of Three Kingdoms, the mastermind and brain truster of the sovereign of the Kingdom of Shu was Zhuge Liang who played a decisive part in Shu's efforts to contend with the other two kingdoms. But Zhuge Liang alone would have achieved nothing without the five valiant generals—Guan Yu, Zhang Fei, Zhao Yun, Ma Chao and Huang Zhong. A good personnel structure was the key to his exploits.

In the Harbin bearings plant, the director and the Party secretary cooperate with each other harmoniously, one taking charge of production and management, the other ideological and political work. They work in unity, mutual respect and coordination, understand each other very well and give each other timely support. And no one of them ever claims credit for himself or shirks his responsibility. All this has contributed much to the smooth progress of things at the plant and its steady growth.

3. Where Prestige of a Commander Comes from

A good leader, as a rule, enjoys high prestige. Prestige reflects the qualities of a leader. It is a force of subtle and imperceptible influence on the minds of the people who accept it readily. Prestige cannot be given by position which gives one power. Power deos not necessarily mean prestige; there are people in high positions who enjoy little or no prestige.

The prestige of a leader comes mainly from what he has achieved in the following three aspects of his life.

(1) Wisdom and moral qualities. In the Warring States Period in Chinese history, the noted strategist Sun Bin who had been mutilated in the state of Wei served as military counseller for Tian Ji, general of the state of Chi. Acting on Sun Bin's advice, Tian Ji led his troops to raise the seige of the state of Zhao by besieging the capital of the state of Wei which was at war with Zhao and in an operation some years later laid ambushes at Maling and doomed Pang Juan, general of the state of Wei, to death. All his orders obeyed faithfully at once, Sun Bin enjoyed unsurpassed reputation and prestige for his "five virtues", his superb resourcefulness and thorough knowledge of the art of war. He knew the need of the people and the balance of power among the states and excelled at making correct judgements and decisions according to the circumstances available and advising the sovereign, the officials, the generals and the soldiers in time about what to do and what to avoid.

(2) Success in the undertakings. Originally a hermit at Longzhong, Zhuge Liang was well known as "the Lying Dragon", but in the eyes of the valiant general Zhang Fei he was but a "village rustic". As military adviser of Liu Bei, sovereign of Shu, who enjoyed his service "as much as a fish enjoys water", Zhuge Liang owed the building of his prestige not to his position, but to his

first scheme of attacking Cao Cao's troops at Xinye by fire which sent them fleeing helter-shelter and earned the admiration and reverence by Zhang Fei, Guan Yu and other general at the same time.

(3) Demeanor of a gifted general. "Sun Zi", ch. 11, "The Nine Varieties of Battleground", states, "Planning his actions, a general should be steady and inscrutable; managing his troops, he should be just and strict". Here, to be steady suggests composure and experienced astuteness; to be inscrutable—unfathomability, dauntlessness before danger and cool-headedness in the presence of a drastic change. A general of great talent should handle things with calmness of his mind and with the help of his rich experience, showing neither joy nor anger in his face. This is a demeanor proper for any manager.

In Chinese history, there was no lack of generals and ministers with such a characteristic demeanor. One of them was Xie An (320-385 A.D.), prime minister of the Eastern Jin Dynasty. According to the chapter entitled "Generosity" of the ancient book "Shishuo Hsinyu" ("A New Account of Tales of the World") written in the fifth century, once Xie An, when a hermit at Dongshan, went boating on the sea with Sun Zhuo, Wang Xizhi and other literary celebrities. Suddenly, a gust sprang up and the waves rose. Sun, Wang and others were seized with panic and exclaimed, "Hurry back to the coast!" But Xie An alone remained in high spirits, singing and chanting as if nothing had happened. Encouraged by Xie An's composure and cheerful expression, the boater rowed forward as before. Only when the wind and the waves turned even more ferocious and people stood up in alarm did Xie An say unhurriedly, "Well, would we go back now?" Back at home, the companions expressed their admiration for Xie, saying that he was a man out of the common run and was capable of great accomplishments as a good governor. And the "History of the Jin Dynasty" relates that after Xie An was made prime minister of the Jin Dynasty, Fu Jian, sovereign of the state of (Former) Chin (in North China), led his 900-thousand-strong army in a large-scale offensive against Jin and reached the area between the Huai River and the Fei River after taking several major towns in succession. Fu Jian declared, "I have so many troops that should each soldier throw his horsewhip into the great Changjiang (Yangtze) River the flowing water could be stopped and held back at once. How could the Jin troops possibly rely on the natural barrier to resist me?" The situation caused alarm among the officials and the people of Jin and panic in the capital city of Jian'an (what is now Nanjing, capital of Jiangsu Province). Only Xie An remained unruffled. He recommended Xie Shi and Xie Xuan, his nephews, to the emperor as commanders of the 80-thousand-strong Jin army to fight the invaders. When Xie Xuan asked him for instruction, he replied only, "There's an imperial decree about it". Xie Xuan waited in silence for some time, feeling it hard to say anything more. When asked by someone sent by Xie Xuan, Xie An gave no reply at all. What was more, he went sight-seeing in a chariot and asked Xue Xuan to play chess with him in his villa. With a load on his mind, Xue Xuan, a player superior to his uncle, found himself locked in a stalemate and finally beat by him. The game being over, Xie An strolled about alone until it was dark. After pondering with a sober mind, he issued his orders and instructions to the generals on returning to his residence that night. And the Jin army won the battle by the Fei River with its inferior forces. When the report of the victory came, Xie An was playing chess with a guest. He was expressionless after reading the report. When asked by the guest how the battle was going on, he replied drily, "The children have crushed the foe". This is what the demeanor of a gifted commander is like, we should say.

Such a demeanor is essential for all managers, and the sports coaches as well. Yuan Weimin, coach of the Chinese women's volleyball team, was never dizzy with success, nor discouraged by failure; he was known to be a man with the demeanor of a gifted commander. In an international tournament held in Japan, the Chinese women's volleyball team met with their U.S. partners and won the five-game match through a bitter struggle to regain the initiative, opening its way to world championship. The Chinese players burst into tears for joy and locked each other into warm embrace, while the spectators broke into deafening cheers, and millions of the Chinese people watching the match televised live by the communications satellite to them were enraptured by the excellent performance of their players. But Yuan Weimin suppressed his excitement, and there was no trace of conceitedness in his face. He was thinking about how to engage the Japanese team the next day and how to plan the future for his team.

The demeanor of a gifted commander should be fostered as part of one's personal character. Here, the hardest thing to do is to put one's emotions under control. It is believed that an experienced manager can keep his temper when he is going to lose it, and fly into a temper when he is in no mood to get angry. It is something of an attainment in personality to determine one's feelings and facial expressions according to the situation instead of one's free will. It differs from hypocrisy or falsehood of heart in that the former is in the interests of the cause one serves while the latter involves personal gains, and the former is the expression of the unity of fine personal qualities with appropriate methods of work while the latter testifies to the height of philistinism.

A manager must learn to control his emotions. If he should let his emotions take the better of him, he is likely to ruin his cause. In the Period of Three Kingdoms, Liu Bei, emperor of Shu, resenting the death of his favourite general Guan Yu at the hands of the troops of Wu, personally led his army in an expedition against Wu, only to be routed by the enemy commander Lu Xun who set Liu's forty and more camps on fire. Soon after that, Liu Bei had to ask his prime minister Zhuge Liang to take care of and assist his heir in his death-bed at Baidicheng. Li Shimin, Emperor Taizong of the Tang Dynasty, led his troops in an expedition against the state of Kokuli in what is now Korea despite the attempts of his ministers to dissuade him. The ambitious, brilliant monarch of the powerful Tang Empire made his best effort, but had to take the bitter fruit of an irrevocable defeat. The reason for his defeat was again failure to control his emotions. "Sun Zi", ch. 12, "Attack by Fire", states, "A sovereign must not raise an army in a fit of anger, nor must a general go into battle in a fit of resentment. Move when it is advantageous to do so; halt when it is not. Anger may be replaced by joy, and resentment by pleasure, but a ruined state can never be restored and the dead be brought back to life. Therefore, the wise sovereign is cautious and the good general is watchful, the way to secure peace for a state and safety for an army". Sun Wu warned the sovereigns and generals not to be driven by their emotion, for it was the interests of the state that should dictate their actions. This is also of cardinal importance to a business manager, for, acting from impulse, he would commit fatal mistakes and endanger the existence and development of his enterprise.

4. Self-Knowledge and Adaptability Needed

As character varies from person to person because of his background, education, temparament and demeanor, a manager has to ask himself how to find out about his character and how to adapt his character to the managerial requirements of his enterprise. Generally, man's character is divided into two types: introvert, or guided, or coordinative type, and extravert, or self-guided, or aggressive type. It is believed that people with a coordinative character are more desirable for the leadership of a growing enterprise, and people with an aggressive character are more competent for the leadership of an enterprise waiting for a change and a new prospect.

As regards the style of leadership, it should likewise vary from enterprise to enterprise, and vary with the size of the enterprises. Some Western scholars hold that there are three styles of leadership: 1. autocratic, when the leader decides on everything and requires absolute obedience of his subordinates; 2. democratic, when the leader consults his subordinates and acts in accordance with the will of the majority; 3. laissez-faire, when the leader gives his subordinates full freedom to do what they wish. Our view is that we should practise a scientific style of leadership with unified direction and decentralized administration on the principle of the unity of democracy and centralism. Both unified direction and decentralized administration should be practised as is required by the occasion. Under the conditions of a socialized big production, unified leadership and command has to be stressed, but the democratic rights of the staff must be respected and exercised adequately, and democracy and centralism must be combined as they should be. Under particular conditions, as in an emergency, the leadership should make its resolute decision in time. In the discussion of major scientific and technological issues which involve a lot of complex factors of professional significance, the leadership should listen carefully to the voices of a lot of people, especially those of the scientific and technological personnel.

In a word, different leaders vary in temparament, character and style of leadership. A wise manager will always remind himself of the necessity of self-control and enhancement of his adaptability, apart from strengthening his self-cultivation. A mediocre commander who sticks to his self and knows no adaptation is not to be recommended.

To be adaptable, a leader must have the wisdom of knowing himself well. Only with the knowledge of his own strong and weak points can he develop his merits and control his demerits and improve his adaptability to meet the challenge of his work as a leader both morally and professionally. "Sun Zi", ch. 3, "The Strategy of Attack", states, "Know the enemy and know yourself, and you can fight a hundred battles with no danger of defeat. When you do not know the enemy but know yourself, you will stand an even chance of winning. If you know neither your enemy nor yourself, danger will keep you company in every battle." From this statement we learn that self-knowledge is as much important as the knowledge of the environment and other people. Only with the knowledge of both your opponents and yourself can you expect to win. And self-knowledge should encompass both your strong and weak points, for a leader's weaknesses in his knowledge, ability, temparament and style of work can also lead to mistakes in making decisions and setbacks in business. A leader's road to success would be through his realizing, controlling and overcoming his faults and demerits while bringing his merits and advantages into full play.

Winding up our book, we would like to cite another story from Chinese history. Zhao Kuo, son of the noted general Zhao She of the state of Zhao in the Warring States Period, learned in his youth the art of war and was so good at talking about war that even his father could not baffle him. But when he took the place of the old general Lian Po as commander of a 400-thousand-strong army, he was crushed by the troops of the state of Chin at Changping. The debacle of the troops of Zhao

Kuo, great talker of war, was due chiefly to his ignorance of flexible use of the principles of the art of war. This book of ours is intended to offer business managers a kind of management method and our armymen of today a guide to their work as business managers of tomorrow and the comrades engaging in the theoretical study of business management a "semi-finished product" to be completed and polished. The feasibility of the management methods offered by this book has to be tested by practice. Knowledge of management is to management of enterprises what learning military works is to getting troops to fight: book learning is necessary, but book knowledge alone is far from being adequate for the practice of management and war alike. As Sun Wu put it well in Chapter 1, "Reckoning", of his treatise, "These belong to the art of a strategist and are beyond any formulation beforehand". Where, then, can we find the key to good business management? In books, and outside books as well —in the practice of men.

Postscript

"Sun Wu's Art of War" is a precious jewel in the treasurehouse of Chinese cultural heritage. This book of ours serves as an initial attempt to apply the scientific ideas, principles and methods offered in the famous military treatise of ancient China to business management and an exploration into the science of business management with Chinese characteristics.

As we failed to find relevant monographs and use them for our reference, and we did not possess enough knowledge and time for our work, the book must contain a number of errors. We hope that readers will not deny us their criticisms and advice.

Our acknowledgement is due to Yunnan Provincial Association of Business Management, Kunming Research Society of Factory Directors and Managers, Guangdong Provincial Research Society of Factory Directors and the Chinese People's University, which have given us support in our work. Our heart-felt thanks is also due to Professor Pan Chenglie from the China Business Management Society, Associate Professor Chen Xun from South China Institute of Technology, Comrade Zhu Fuchang from the Guangdong Provincial Research Society of Factory Directors, lecturer Dai Tianquan from the Kunming Institute of Technology and Comrade Zhao Zhonghou, deputy commander of the Xishuangbanna military subarea of Yunnan Province, who have favoured us with their warm-hearted help.

Writing our book, we have greatly benefited from consulting "Sun Zi with Annotations by Eleven Scholars" printed by Shanghai Ancient Works Publishing House and other books on "Sun Wu's Art of War", and "Business Management in

China's Socialist Industry" compiled by the Chinese People's University and other books on management. We owe them a debt of gratitude and appreciation.

The Authors
June 1984, Kunming